THE FOURTH FRONTIER

THE FOURTH

EXPLORING THE NEW WORLD OF WORK

FRONTIER

STEPHEN R. GRAVES AND
THOMAS G. ADDINGTON

WORD PUBLISHING
NASHVILLE
A Thomas Nelson Company

Unless otherwise noted, Scripture quotations are from the Holy Bible: New International Version®. Copyright ©1973, 1978, 1984 by International Bible Society. Used by permission of Zondervan Publishing House. All rights reserved.

Scripture quotations marked TLB are from The Living Bible, copyright © 1971. Used by permission of Tyndale House Publishers, Inc., Wheaton, Illinois 60189. All rights reserved.

Library of Congress Cataloging-in-Publication Data

Graves, Stephen R., 1955–
    The fourth frontier : discovering God in your work / by Stephen R. Graves and Thomas G.
  Addington.
      p. cm.
  ISBN 0-8499-1668-2
  1. Stewardship, Christian. 2. Work—Religious aspects—Christianity. I. Addington, Thomas G., 1955– II. Title.
  BV772.G68 2000
  248.8'8—dc21   00-
043319

                                                                              CIP

Printed in the United States of America
00 01 02 03 04 05 06 BVG 6 5 4 3 2 1

———

To our heroes—
the men and women practitioners of the faith
in the marketplace around the world

———

CONTENTS

ACKNOWLEDGMENTS

This book has been more like a community potluck social than a pair of cooks working together in the kitchen. How so? Well, a number of skilled and talented friends and professionals contributed here and there along the way, some offering huge portions to the main course and others simply adding the much-needed spices to bring out the flavor of the meal.

Thanks to Sean Womack, our founding partner in The Life@Work Co., for your help and friendship. You moved us from Ecclesiastes 4:9 to Ecclesiastes 4:12.

Thanks to Stephen Caldwell, our executive editor at Life@Work, Dianna Booher, and Rob Wilkins for your help in writing the manuscript.

Thanks to Howard Hendricks, Bob Buford, Bill Pollard, Os Guinness, Doug Sherman, and Robert Lewis for helping us shape ideas, perhaps without your even knowing it.

Thanks to Grant Nelson for believing in the Life@Work vision before anyone else. To Steve Griffin, COO of the Life@Work Company, for bringing his organizational gifts to Life@Work enterprises.

Thanks to the Board of Directors and the Board of Advisors of Life@Work for guiding the Life@Work ship through some tough waters in the early part of our journey.

Thanks to our team at Life@Work for helping to create the laboratory for this discussion.

Thanks to Tonya Sites for handling so much of the transcription work, and to Clay Bell for his help with the research.

Thanks to our friends at Word Publishing, especially Mark Sweeney, Ami McConnell, and Holly Parker Halverson for your faith in the book and your help in editing the manuscript.

Thanks to Greg Johnson at Alive Communications for guiding us into the book publishing world.

And thanks to our families—Karen, Katelyn, Julianne, and Kile; Susan, Kim, Sally, and Joel—for allowing us to add another task to our already rigorous workload.

PART I

THE CASE FOR WORK—
THE JOURNEY BEGINS

THE FOURTH FRONTIER:
CLAIMING YOUR FUTURE

FERDINAND MAGELLAN HAD *every reason to celebrate when he and his small fleet reached Cape Virgennes on the southern tip of South America and found what previously existed in the European world only as a rumor—a westward water passage into what he would name the Pacific Ocean.*

It was October 21, 1520, more than a year after Magellan had set sail from Spain with five ships and a crew of more than 250 men. He had survived a grueling winter and a mutiny that cost him three officers. But his fierce determination, his faith in God and in his mission, and his loyalty to the king of his adopted country was about to pay off. Soon he would make the northwestern trek to what were known as the Spice Islands and establish a profitable new trade route with Asia on behalf of King Carlos of Spain.

Or so he thought.

Little did Magellan know that the testing of that determination, faith, and loyalty had just begun. By the time he navigated the stormy seas of the 373-mile channel, one of his ships had secretly deserted and returned to Spain.

To this development Magellan responded with a familiar cry: "Sail on; sail on." It was an order that his crew would hear again and again; the size of this newfound ocean had been greatly underestimated. Fighting fear, fatigue, frustration, and hunger, Magellan and his men survived three months on the open seas, feeding on rats, ox hides, and sawdust before reaching what now is known as Guam.

From there, Magellan discovered the archipelago of San Lazaro (the Philippines), where he planned to rest his men, repair his ships, and restock his galleys before moving on to his original destination.

Magellan's first encounters with the natives of the Philippines were positive. Eight days after his arrival, the Catholic captain baptized an island chief and several hundred islanders. But in a battle with neighboring islanders, a poisoned arrow felled Magellan. He died April 27, 1521.

With their captain's words whispering in the wind, "Sail on; sail on," the crews of two ships completed the journey to the Spice Islands. One attempted to return via the Pacific route, but the Portuguese captured and imprisoned its men. The other, the Victoria, reached Spain on September 8, 1522, with a crew of eighteen and more than enough spices to pay the expenses of the three-year voyage.

More important, the voyage changed forever the dynamics of economic trade in a suddenly round world. Magellan, an outcast in his native country of Portugal, was, in the words of Os Guinness, "a dreamer fired by an inner vision and fortified by devout faith."[1] He had recognized an external opportunity: the chance to explore and discover an awaiting new world. And he had pursued it with a fierce inward sense of loyalty and determination on behalf of King Carlos. He had followed his orders, despite long odds and difficult times. And he had conquered an unknown frontier.

A New Frontier for a New Millennium

A new territory lies at the rim of the New Economy. This territory has been around since the beginning of time but in many ways is as uncharted and foreign to followers of Christ in the twenty-first century as the South Pacific was to Magellan and his shipmates during the sixteenth. It's the territory of work. We call it the Fourth Frontier.

Like Magellan, we aggressively approach this frontier with two primary motives: the outward observation that it's ripe with opportunity and the inward realization that we're commanded to do so by our King.

In addition to the worlds of family, government, and church, God has created this Fourth Frontier for us to explore, discover, and cultivate for his glory. Many followers of Jesus have access to a great deal of information about three of those institutions—the church, the government, and the family. We understand that the church is nothing less than the body of Christ, directed by God to love him, each other, and the lost. The need for strong families has received a great deal of attention in recent years with the rise of such invaluable ministries as Focus on the Family, Promise Keepers, and FamilyLife. Clearly, God mandates the investment of our lives into the lives of our spouses and children. Christians, too, are active in government, working diligently for the passage of laws supporting biblical values.

But what about work? What sermons have we heard lately about the inherent value and beauty of work? Mysteriously, an aura of silence surrounds the God-ordained institution of work, often leaving modern-day explorers disoriented and puzzled.

Such was the case with Barry Logan (not his real name), who was making $160,000 as senior vice president at an insurance company. During Christmas week, he got a call from his boss, who happened to double as his golf buddy. "Barry, I'm afraid I've got some bad news. I hate to deliver it during the Christmas season, but I guess there's never a good time for this sort of thing."

Barry's chest tightened. "So, shoot. What's up?"

"We've decided to do away with your position. We can give you thirty days to find a new job."

"You mean a new job inside—some other area? But why?"

"No." There was a long pause. "Outside."

Barry let the "why" part of his question drop. What did it matter? He hung up the phone and sank onto the sofa. How could he tell Rochelle and the kids after what they'd just been through? The decision to move to Atlanta for the new job a year ago had been tough, but all of them eventually had agreed that it was the right thing for the family. He'd pulled Rochelle and his twelve- and sixteen-year-old boys out of Mississippi, where they'd been surrounded by three generations of relatives. For what? For this? It didn't make any sense.

Stunned, Barry sat silently for a long hour while he replayed the last year of his life. He racked his brain for clues that this was coming.

The company chiefs in Atlanta had told Barry he had a great opportunity to make "tons of money." That part had been correct. The company was making money hand over fist. Barry's own division was doubling revenues every quarter. So how could he personally be so expendable? How could he be booted off the top rung? What base didn't he touch? He'd built a network, fit in, socialized. And it wasn't as though he'd just moved into their territory and collected a contribution; he'd grown the company through the curve.

Performance evaluations from years past rolled through Barry's mind.

Excellent, every one. Every job. Was it even about him? Big corporations often laid off employees at year-end to improve the bottom line and then rehired them three months later. Didn't they realize the impact these kinds of reversals had on families?

The biggest confusion: How could he have been so far off in reading God's direction? Barry had been sure God had moved them, had given him the perfect job for his skills and previous experience, had put him in the perfect place to raise a family. No, he'd never worked just for a paycheck. He felt as though he was being salt and light in his marketplace.

So why this? He just wanted to know. The dismissal struck at the very core of his self-worth.

To this day, Barry is searching for the answers.

Only the Sturdy Need Apply

The Fourth Frontier: It's no journey for the weak-kneed and fainthearted.

As Barry Logan discovered, it can be an unforgiving terrain. And the traditional sources for faith-based answers to life's dilemmas often fail to recognize the existence of the territory, much less make efforts to provide direction for getting through it. When mentioned at all, work generally is viewed as negative, something that keeps us from spending our time and energy on truly *important* issues—family and church. Even our daily conversations color work with negative brush strokes:

"TGIF—do I ever need a weekend."

"Wednesday is hump day—I'm halfway through."

"Sorry, can't go to the ball game; I've got to work."

"Remember that all work and no play makes Jack a dull boy."

"Work is just killing me."

"I'm on a treadmill, and I can't get off."

"There's no meaning to my work; it's just a paycheck."

At best, many followers of Christ, uninformed or misinformed about what the Bible teaches regarding work, simply treat it as a necessity, something they must do to make a living—a separate, disconnected activity of existence. Work is from nine to five on Monday through Friday, and *real* life—the good life—happens all the rest of the time.

A case in point: I (Steve) was having breakfast with a few friends. All three were believers who work in "secular" professions. Over the omelettes, one told us about a book he was reading and then said, "A book like that makes me realize what a lousy job I'm doing in evangelizing my neighborhood. I just don't share my faith often enough."

The other two joined in. In a nutshell, their comments came down to this: "We're not doing enough that has eternal significance. We're not making a difference in the world."

"Whoa," I spoke up. "If anybody's being salt and light in this world, it's you three guys." As I went on to explain what I'd observed in their lives through the years, their expressions changed from gloom to glee. As husbands and fathers, these men were making an incredible impression on their families. As church leaders, they were having a deep impact on their community. And as a physician, a dentist, and a businessman, they were influencing clients, patients, vendors, staff, and colleagues on a daily basis. Furthermore, each life they touched created a ripple effect that was immeasurable. They were stunned. They'd never considered their jobs as their platform for ministry, their calling, their method of influencing the world for God's kingdom.

What happens when we dismiss work, a significant and critical part of our day, as less important than the rest of our time? And what if that less important time just happens to be—by sheer number of hours—the place we spend most of our waking time? What does our attitude say about our view of God? Is he less present at a conference table at Smith, Jones, Ramseyer & Whitmer than he is at a church Communion service or at our dinner table?

So Where Are We Going?

The thesis of this book is simple: God has ordained work. It was his idea. Whether you are a man or a woman, twenty-five or fifty-five, conservative or liberal, wealthy or poor, work is a critical part of your life. You spend eighty thousand to one hundred thousand of your best hours there. If you don't see work as God-ordained, you miss the opportunities to mature and experience fulfillment that God has placed there. There should be a seamless connection between Friday and Sunday and between Sunday and Monday.

By giving work such a high status with a newfangled name as the Fourth Frontier, we understand the implications. The old mission, to survive in a marketplace that has no relevance to the deeper meaning of life, often is filled with inaccurate maps and limited vocabulary. It simply will not take us to the New World, where an integrated life leaves no areas untouched by faith. In fact, these maps may make us miss a wealth of possibilities altogether. In order to explore the Fourth Frontier successfully, we need to understand our specific mission. And we should not travel unprepared.

Like Magellan, followers of Christ have a King who has issued a decree. Our King, the God of the cosmos, has given us a wealth of information and maps for exploring the Fourth Frontier; he has outlined our responsibilities in his *Magna Carta*—the Scriptures. He has invested gifts in us for expression and worship that must be exercised in the work world. His decree is to be salt to an unseasoned, decaying culture and light to a dark, dangerous world.

But that's not all. Besides the internal sense of responsibility to our King, we have an unprecedented external opportunity for delivering that salt and light. The cultural doors of the postmodern world are swinging open—in some cases have already swung open—and it is now up to followers of Christ, individually and collectively, to come in, explore the terrain, and establish a kingdom influence in the marketplace.

British essayist Dorothy Sayers explained it this way: "In nothing has the church so lost her hold on reality as in her failure to understand and respect the secular vocation, she has allowed work and religion to become separate departments. . . . She has forgotten that the secular vocation is sacred."[2]

And if the church no longer sees work as sacred, is it any wonder that so many workers no longer see their faith as sacred? "How can anyone remain interested in a religion," asked Sayers, "that seems to have no concern with nine-tenths of life?"[3]

A few years ago Doug Sherman and William Hendricks wrote a groundbreaking book called *Your Work Matters to God*. At this stage, it is critical to understand that the reverse is equally true—God matters to your work! Accepting and combining those two big ideas is the first step toward leading an integrated life in the Fourth Frontier.

The exploration begins here, with this book. As we launch, consider your own attitudes about work.

- Do you feel passionate about your work? As older workers retire, they often ask, "Did all the energy and effort I put into my career really matter to anyone?" Baby boomers are moving toward their midlife question, "How do I want to spend the second half of my career?" Generation Xers are asking, "Is it important to go to work today? Will it count? Is this project meaningful?"

- Do you feel pulled in opposite directions—that work takes you away from family or church?

- Do you ever feel that there are just not enough hours in the day to accomplish all God has asked you to do?

- Is your work significant for God's kingdom?

- Have you been led to believe that the only ministry that really "counts" is done inside the church or in a parachurch organization?

- Do you ever feel "compromised" at work, that you're not really taking a stand and being biblical salt and light in your marketplace?

- Do you ever feel guilty that you're enjoying prosperity?

If these questions raise more questions and even doubts, we invite you along for the journey of self-discovery about your stake in the Fourth Frontier.

But be warned. This is not a self-help book. There is no seven-step formula to a better work life. Our focus will be what we call "realities"—realities of someone settling in the Fourth Frontier. But the exploration by each pioneer in the Fourth Frontier will be unique. We are all at different places in our walk with Jesus. We possess different skill sets. And we have different expertise and platforms in the business world. But that's what exploration entails: a creative adventure in your own space shuttle, seafaring ship, or Yukon kayak.

What we hope to provide is some work-specific vocabulary from God's Word, to outline some general attitudes and motivations, and to show, in a broad manner, what the integration of work and faith might look like: six realities common in those who do well by God's standards in the Fourth Frontier. By focusing on the lives of some truly cutting-edge explorers, we can provide some different models of how Christianity can take shape on the job.

At the end of our journey together, we can promise that you'll be well on your way to:

- understanding God's personal calling for your life;

- experiencing a sense of satisfaction and a God-connection to your job;

- using your God-given skills for his kingdom *while* you're at work;

- feeling passion, peace, and purpose about your time between nine and five;

- avoiding the typical fears and anxieties that strangle joy for the average worker;

- creating a supportive synergy between your family and your work life;

- feeling balance in all areas of your life—a composite score of "well done."

The Misunderstood Territory

Magellan lived in a time when many people still believed the earth was flat, that to sail in any one direction for too long would take you and your ship right off the edge and into the fire-filled, bottomless pit of hell. The Wright brothers built an airplane when the common thinking of the day was: "If God intended men to fly, he would have given them wings." Neil Armstrong set foot on the moon in an era when many thought space exploration was a violation of God's command to "inhabit the earth." The Fourth Frontier is no less shackled by the chains of misconception. Consider these commonly held myths connected to work:

Myth 1: Work is a four-letter word

It is part of God's curse, delivered in anger by the Creator after Adam and Eve directly disobeyed him in the Garden of Eden. Those who embrace this myth see work as a career-long punishment that all of us—past, present, and future—must endure because Adam and Eve bought into Satan's great lie. The truth is that work was one of God's first assignments for Adam. Like the family, work is "a creation ordinance"—a blessing and an assignment.

Myth 2: Work is enemy territory

It is part of the secular world, not to be confused with the sacred world. "God-stuff" includes such things as prayer, Bible study, worship services, and donations of time and money to worthy "ministries." Work is secular.

This approach is totally counter to Scripture. This dichotomy—this split between the sacred and the secular—doesn't occur in God's Word. In fact, Scripture spends a good deal of ink and paper making the point that these two should be tied together—that work is part of God's everyday involvement with people.

Myth 3: Work is salvation

For people who buy into this myth, work becomes God. They don't go to work; they go to Work. They don't seek success; they seek Success. They don't have ambition; they have Ambition. Their entire identity becomes wrapped up in their job. This is a particularly dangerous side of a "work is the family" culture, so much a part of the New Economy. Many organizations, religious or otherwise, sell a family-oriented culture as a benefit. And it can be. People who take this idea to the extreme can become emotional and spiritual prisoners to their jobs. The difference between what we called workaholism in the eighties and feeling passionate about your work in the new millennium is one of motivation. Workaholism has no place in the Fourth Frontier. The truth is that work is a great environment in which to discover God and to glorify God, but it is *not* God.

Myth 4: Work is the last priority

Many followers of Christ, if asked to list their priorities, would order them this way: God, family, self, and work. The fact is an integrated holistic view of life *includes* work. Consider a new set of priorities for life: God. That's it. There is no number two or number three or number four. In living out a commitment to that priority, we must make him an integrated part of everything we do—family, self, and work.

Besides, relegating work to caboose status is as impractical as it is unbiblical. If we really put work *last*, we would not leave for work each day until we had done *everything* we should for God, family, and self. We'd never earn a living! No, the truth is that work is part of a balanced approach to life and God—his Spirit, his truth, his love. God shouldn't be left behind in the family Bible on the nightstand next to the comfy chair where we have our daily quiet time.

The Rapidly Changing Territory

All kinds of shifts affect the conversation of work and faith, just as all kinds of shifts affect the planet we live on. During a recent trip to Nevis in the Caribbean, we were walking with our spouses around the end of the island that connected the gulf with the Atlantic Ocean. We suddenly found ourselves hitting a dead end—a washed-up area where the beach and the land had collided to form cliffs that cut our walk short. After talking to some locals, we discovered that until Hurricane George had hit the islands, it had been possible to walk around that end of the island from the Caribbean to the Atlantic Ocean. But the currents of the channels had changed; the hurricane had reconstructed the landscape of the tiny island of Nevis.

In the Fourth Frontier, there is a shift toward the soft side of business. A few years ago the only criterion for success was delivering results. Now most companies are looking for someone who can deliver results *and* build people. The path to the CEO suite used to be through the finance or accounting departments. Then it shifted to the sales and marketing departments. Now if someone wants to rise to the higher echelons of the company, he or she must have people skills.

Another shift in the Fourth Frontier is the surge of Bible- or morality-based, principle-driven technology. John Grisham's bestseller *The Testament* attests to this. "This is the same John Grisham we've always known," the host of a national talk show said to Grisham, "only there is a new character in your book, and the new character is God." Ten years ago, Grisham's agent might have shuddered to think that God and/or Bible-based conversation would play a significant role in a plot for this famous mega-author. Yet In 1999 the *Los Angeles Times* ran a fifty-page special section on spirituality in the workplace; *BusinessWeek* ran a cover story on religion and work; *Fast Company*, which focuses on holistic solutions to work, became the hottest business magazine in the mainstream market; and *The Life@Work Journal*, which centers on the integration of faith and work, began its second year of publication.

There is a move toward total-solution strategies to life. Every sliding generation, from the Builders to the Boomers to the Busters to the Bridgers, has less tolerance for a schizophrenic, polarized lifestyle. Each generation longs for a more holistic approach to life.

Media and entertainment also reflect this change. The neocommunity is work, not family. Compare the top TV shows of past generations with the top TV shows in this generation. Shows such as *Leave It to Beaver, Happy Days, All in the Family,* and *Dallas* centered on the family. Most of the top TV shows of the late nineties and early 2000 center on work with family woven in as the subplot: *ER, Frasier, Just Shoot Me, Caroline in the City, Ally McBeal, The Practice, NYPD Blue.* We see the change even within one ongoing series: *The Cosby Show* of the eighties focused on Bill's family; the *Cosby* show of the nineties focused on his work. There are exceptions, of course. But by and large, where the media once looked at culture and saw it in the home, it now looks at culture and sees it at work.

The Uniquely Positioned Territory

More than twenty years ago a businessman visiting Mississippi College predicted an interesting trend that made a lasting impact on me (Steve). The evangelist of the nineties, he said, will be the Christian businessperson. That speaker could see the new platform for ministry beginning to take shape, and today his prediction has come true.

> It is the marketplace that carries the traffic of a lost world.

According to an article in *USA Today,* "In the 21st century, more religious leaders will be found in the corporation than in the conventional church."[4] *BusinessWeek* announced: "A spiritual revival is sweeping across Corporate America" and "gone is the old taboo against talking about God at work."[5] William Pollard, chairman of $5.7 billion ServiceMaster, put it this way: In today's global community, the greatest channel of distribution for salt and light is the business community, the marketplace.

The horizon is full of promise and potential. If we can learn to be the persons God wants us to be in the frontier of work, we can unleash an enormous amount of God's power into the world. What would happen if 100 million followers of Jesus began to understand what he desires from them at the workplace? Can you imagine the integrity, professionalism, skill, love, forgiveness, service that could come into play? It is the marketplace that carries the traffic of a lost world.

Imagine, too, the benefits that each of us might find. As we discover (or rediscover) the Fourth Frontier, we find a rhythm of family, church, government, and work and begin to understand the kind of life God has in mind for each of his beloved—a life of hope, purpose, abundance, and wholeness.

The Waiting Territory

The Raid Gauloises is considered by many to be the most rigorous and challenging expedition in the world. Participants compete in some of the most extreme sporting activities known to man: rafting, canoeing, horseback riding, camel riding, dugout canoeing, sea kayaking, rock climbing, skydiving, hang gliding, mountain biking, running, and plain old swimming. In 1998, the competition included climbing a six-thousand-meter volcano in Ecuador. In 2000, it started in Tibet and finished in India.

The Raid Gauloises usually lasts about ten days, and the rules are simple. Teams of five competitors (both men and women) and two assistants work together to race across whatever rough terrain—mountains, jungles, lakes, and rivers—the organizers have put before them. There is more than one available route, but there are checkpoints along the way. Physical fitness is not the only quality required of team members. According to the event's organizers, "Solidarity with the group and being able to adapt, anticipate and know one's limits are indispensable."[6]

The team that gets to the finish first is declared the winner, but the race is about more than winning. "Personal growth is far more important . . . than competition," the organizers say. "Indeed, setting out on the Raid Gauloises is the ultimate adventure." Finishing requires planning, vision, and teamwork. It pushes the participants beyond every comfort zone, forcing them to engage in thrilling but emotionally and intellectually draining challenges. It is advertised as "a start and a finish. Between the two, a great experience!"[7] And while we personally haven't taken part, we suspect it delivers on the promise.

But the Raid Gauloises comes and goes every year. Organizers must find new locations, new challenges, new feats; to deliver against their promises. And no more than forty-five teams participate each year. It is limited to those with the time, the desire, and the money.

The Fourth Frontier, on the other hand, is open to everyone. For followers of Christ, it is the *real* ultimate adventure. Work is assigned by God, whether paid or volunteer effort, whether you're doing the family laundry or designing a corporate merger. Work forces participants out of their comfort zones, challenging them to engage in thrilling but emotionally and intellectually draining feats. And like the Raid Gauloises, work requires a variety of skills and talents.

Participation isn't optional, not for disciples of Jesus. It's a biblical mandate. Followers of Jesus must embrace the challenge to engage in the greatest opportunity for kingdom influence the world has ever known. The marketplace. The Fourth Frontier.

PREPARING FOR THE TRIP:
YOUR THEOLOGY OF WORK

In 1583, GALILEO Galilei was distracted from his prayers by the swinging of an altar lamp in the cathedral of Pisa. He was struck by a curiosity: No matter how wide the swing of the lamp, the time it took for the lamp to swing from one side to the other seemed the same. He crudely confirmed his suspicion by measuring the intervals with his pulse. He had, in fact, made a critical discovery, which physicists would later name isochronism—the reality that the time of a pendulum's swing does not vary with the swing's width. Springing from this principle came the invention of the clock and the ability, for the first time in history, to precisely and universally mark time.

At nearly the same time, the magnetic compass, with its mysterious power to point in only one direction, was shedding its aura of mystery and occult. Previously used in rituals of fortunetelling, divination, and necromancy, the lodestone ("the stone that leads") had been used for navigational purposes in China as early as A.D. 1000. But on the continent of Europe, it was locked—sometimes literally—in a box of superstition for the next six hundred years. Even small pieces of the mineral were once considered to have great and dark power—to heal disease, prevent pregnancy, and, under the pillow of an unfaithful wife, force confession of sin. During the previous three or four centuries, sea captains often hid the small floating needle in its own binnacle, or "little house," to keep their superstitious crews from anxiety and sometimes mutiny.

Eventually, the compass's necessity overruled all objections to its use. Without the compass, space was relative, marked primarily by the movement of the sun and winds. On overcast and still days you were, technically speaking, quite lost. The compass became the accepted navigational standard shortly after the invention of the mechanical clock. Man was now capable of marking himself in both time and space.

Daniel Boorstin, *author of* The Discoverers, *summed up the importance of this step forward for mankind:*

> *In practice the compass provided a worldwide absolute for space comparable to that which the mechanical clock and the uniform hour provided for time. . . . From the very nature of our spherical spinning planet, the marking of time and the marking of space were inseparable. When you moved any great distance from home out into the uncharted great oceans, you could not know precisely where you were unless you had a way of precisely finding when you were. Locating yourself on the whole planet meant finding your place on the grid of latitudes and longitudes.*[1]

Together, the clock and the compass led to a golden age of exploration and discovery that continues into outer space.

The Golden Age of Discovery Continues

In the first few weeks of his job as a medical equipment salesman, Larry Watkins faced a number of dilemmas he had never experienced in his previous eleven years as a youth pastor.

Like the time he was about to attempt his first sale: driving across rural Arkansas to a one-doctor town, he caught himself saying aloud, "Lord, what am I going to do if I don't make this sale? How can we make the mortgage? What if I don't make it in this job?"

He pulled up to the rustic-looking building, got out with a deliberate show of confidence, and pushed his way through the sticking screen door. The nurse-receptionist in overalls took his name and told him the doctor would see him when he finished with his patients. As he took a seat, Larry surveyed the makeshift waiting room; he saw a pregnant teenager and a couple in their eighties, holding hands. *Could be awhile,* he thought. He picked up a magazine and pretended to read.

Maybe he should get another job. Why had he thought he could sell? Why the medical field? Maybe he should try another industry. Would Gwen understand if he came home empty-handed? The only thing that seemed certain was that he had to make this sale. He silently uttered a simple prayer: "Lord, I'm doing the best I know how to provide for my family. Please—I really need your help."

The nurse finally spoke from behind the counter. "The doctor will see you now." Obediently, Larry followed her down the hallway. "Lord, please let him buy one—that'll come close to covering the mortgage. Just one, that's all I ask."

The doctor came around the desk and shook his hand. "What have you got there?" Larry opened his secondhand sales bag and demonstrated the instrument. Almost before he could finish his practiced pitch, the doctor responded, "I'll take two. If I sign the paperwork today, how soon can I have them? Can you ship them immediately?"

Larry whipped out the paperwork, trying to suppress the urge to make a touchdown yell. On the drive home, he phoned Gwen, so overwhelmed that he could hardly talk. His earlier sense of desperation was matched only by God's disarming call, "Trust me."

There were other tests of Larry's new calling as a salesman—for instance, the day his new boss asked him to lie. "Look, here's what you've got to do," his boss said to him. "Your accounts are just like mine. Those hospitals don't keep good enough records to know what they ordered and what they didn't. Don't they let you basically handle their inventory for them?"

Larry conceded, "Yeah, sure. They do."

"So load 'em up," his boss said, as if it were a done deal. "If you can stock them up with another two thousand dollars' worth, you'll meet your quota for the month. We'll meet *our* quota for the month. And we'll all live happily ever after."

"But they don't need the stuff," Larry insisted. "They've got a full inventory. They didn't order the product. They don't need it—I just can't do it."

"Why not? I do it all the time. They'll never notice. Nobody will. Just you and me." Larry's boss paused, turned his tone to pleading. "Hey, my neck's on the line. We've got to make quota."

Larry stood there, his mind spinning. He knew that if he insisted on the truth, his boss would see him as uncooperative, defiant. He argued with himself: couldn't he afford, for the sake of getting off to a good start with him, just to carry off the deal, just this once? Surely the hospital would eventually use all that stuff. After all, it wouldn't rot on the shelf or anything like that.

"Just this month," his boss pressed. "Next month, the numbers will look better. I've got several accounts just ready to close. But this month, we just need to push 'em a little. What do you say?"

"I just can't do it, that's all." In Larry's heart were the clock and compass for moral direction.

The Way the Clock and Compass Work Today

To repeat: Businesspeople will be the evangelists of the future. The reasons are obvious. First, the majority of people's time is spent in the workplace. If we're going to get spiritual seekers' attention, we're going to have to meet them there. Second, the workplace presents the situations and holds the energy to demonstrate God in everyday life. Third, the moral agenda of the culture now demands a spiritual answer to life's issues. Fourth, businesspeople have ready entrée to seekers. They've already built solid relationships with nonbelievers in the workplace. Fifth, businesspeople have credibility with their colleagues because of demonstrated expertise and relevant experience. They can say to a nonbeliever, "I understand. I've been there. The Bible is relevant. God works."

In his foreknowledge of our twenty-first-century world, Jesus prepared believers for the workplace. Of his forty recorded parables, more than half concern economic matters or are situated in a marketplace context. Consider the parable of the vineyard, the parable of the shrewd manager, the parable of the talents, of the lost sheep, of the coins, of the rich young ruler, of the mustard seed. These teachings contain a working theology, work strategies, for all followers of Christ.

More than half of Jesus' parables contain a working theology, work strategies, for all followers of Christ.

They Call It "Paradise"

When you think of the word *paradise,* what comes to mind? What images, what color and texture of words does your mind choose to paint the perfect picture? How about this: lying under the stars in the Rockies, a spring-fed river running nearby with tomorrow's trout, your family asleep, a campfire as slow and silver-orange as the full moon.

Or maybe this: crawling up the first, great hill of a roller coaster named "Rampage" or "The Beast" or "Scorpion," your heart pumping, pupils dilated, arms extended, adrenaline surging, and then down, freefall of steel and flesh, synapses exploding, weightless, all skin, rushing wind and voices, the all-out obliteration of sensation—pure thrill!

Then again: early morning cup of coffee in front of a Christmas tree, Nat King Cole in the background, a box of chocolates ready, the whispering promises of something good about to get even better.

Or try this: you and your spouse, in a room lit by candles with a Jacuzzi . . . well, maybe we'd better not go *precisely* there, but you get the idea.

One final try: Monday morning, behind a desk with a ringing phone and a frozen computer and an unsmiling assistant—if you are lucky enough to have one—who happens to be asking you for time off while papers spill onto the floor, and the boss wants to see the finished presentation in exactly fifty-seven minutes and thirty-three seconds.

For most Americans, the ideas of work and paradise are as related as ice fishing and Jamaica. They might as well be antonyms, buzzing with the opposing energy of an oxymoron: freezer burn, jumbo shrimp, and working paradise. In fact, most of the cultural perceptions of paradise are strikingly marked by the *absence* of work: travel brochures, retirement magazines, and lottery advertisements. Work, we are led to believe, is at best a chore, a duty, or a way to pay the bills.

> For most Americans, the idea of work and paradise are as related as ice fishing and Jamaica.

How do we explain, then, that work first appears in the Garden of Eden, in the very heart of the paradise God created for humans?

Labor Pains

Many contemporary followers of Christ believe the Garden of Eden was a place without work and that "labor" was introduced by God as a punishment for Adam's sin. The often difficult nature of work is seen to be proof positive of its inherent role as the activity of humans *after* the Fall. In other words, if we had not sinned, work would not exist. Paradise, once again, unstained by work. This idea carries tremendous implications. A person's theology greatly determines how he or she lives life: with fear or freedom, hopelessness or purpose, humility or pride. What we believe directly affects what we do.

C. S. Lewis, the brilliant Christian apologist, wisely wrote, "Correct thinking will not make good men of bad ones; but a purely theoretical error may remove ordinary checks to evil and deprive good intentions of their natural support."[2] The person who believes work is the curse of God and the person who believes that work is a potential blessing of God will walk to his or her workplace with different struts, accomplishing fundamentally dissimilar goals.

So what does the Bible teach about work? Is it a fundamental experience of life, designed to yield purpose, development, and service to God and others? Or is it a tedious punishment that we must simply seek to endure until we outlive it or graduate?

Genesis 3:14–19 records the three curses of God for the serpent, for Eve, and for Adam. The third curse is certainly connected to the idea of work:

> "Cursed is the ground because of you;
>> through painful toil you will eat of it
>> all the days of your life.
> It will produce thorns and thistles for you,
>> and you will eat the plants of the field.
> By the sweat of your brow
>> you will eat your food
> until you return to the ground,
>> since from it you were taken;
> for dust you are
>> and to dust you will return." (Gen. 3:17–19)

Later, in verse 23, the Bible says of Adam: "So the LORD God banished him from the Garden of Eden to work the ground from which he had been taken."

Indeed, work—in some sense—has been cursed; at the very least, it will be difficult and often filled with pain, toil, and frustration. But to say that work suffers somehow under a curse is a different thing altogether from saying work *is* the curse. That would be like confusing a bent nail for a hammer. Work was not the only human activity singled out for the curse. In the second curse, outlined in verse 16, childbirth also would become a difficult experience: to Eve—and all women after her—God said he would "greatly increase [her] pains." God did not curse childbearing itself but rather made it "labor." The curse was the pain, not the concept of childbearing. Otherwise, there is no sanctity of life. If God cursed childbearing, at the sound of a newborn's cry we should feel despair, not joy.

God already had ordained work before the Fall. Genesis 2:15 reads, "The LORD God took the man and put him in the Garden of Eden to *work it and take care of it*" (emphasis added). The time frame is critical; God placed man, the bearer of his own image, in the garden at the conclusion of the six days of creation. The work of man followed and was to mimic a pattern of work that God conceived and practiced: six days of work, a day of rest. In the rhythm of work and rest, God established a fundamental principle of life on earth as integral as the laws of physics.

> To say that work suffers somehow under a curse is a different thing altogether from saying work is the curse. That would be like confusing a bent nail for a hammer.

As designed by God, work was not just something for man to do—a sort of cosmic aerobics class—but amazingly, a deep participation in the life and work of God himself. The purpose was to "take care" of the earth, to steward it. That mandate for work did not change after the Fall; indeed, with God pulling out of direct fellowship with man, it could be argued that its role constitutes the central imperative. The issue of stewardship—that man is entrusted with taking care of God's resources in the same manner he would—is the lynchpin of understanding a theology of work.

The fact is, work played a key role in the original, and only real, earthly paradise. This is bad news for those who prefer to imagine Eden *sans* the nine-to-five. But it gets worse. Heaven—our future paradise—also will involve work in some form. Compare Genesis 3:17 to Revelation 22:3, bookends of the Bible: the first says, as we saw earlier, "Cursed is the ground because of you; through painful toil you will eat of it." The second: "No longer will there be any curse. The throne of God and of the Lamb will be in the city, and his servants will serve him."

From a biblical and eternal perspective, retirement—the cessation of work—exists only in the concept and practice of the Sabbath. Many people, even though they still could be productive, quit being so. But in God's plan a person's influence does not stop at age sixty-five. If you doubt, consider this: Does the institution of family stop? Does your role as spouse or parent stop at some set age? And how about the institution of church—do you stop going to church to worship at a certain age? God gave us gifts to be used at church and in the service of humankind in the community and workplace, and they have no expiration date.

That doesn't mean, of course, that work constitutes the same duties at all ages. For example, we function one way in our role as parents when our kids are living at home with us than we do when they're gone and have families of their own. Our role as a husband or wife is one thing when we have toddlers at home and another when we have an empty nest. So, of course, our role in work will go through similar transitions. But the idea that all productive work should stop at some mandated age is no more biblical than that our roles in the home, at church, or in government should cease.

> The idea that all productive work should stop at some mandated age is no more biblical than that our roles in the home, at church, or in government should cease.

Listening to God individually becomes paramount in understanding the work, paid or voluntary, and the ministry platform of influence he has for us throughout our lives.

Full-time Ministry

When Larry Watkins left his job as a youth pastor, he believed he was leaving "the ministry" behind him. It was, in many ways, a painful transition. At the time, the church's pastor had left, and in the wake the elders decided to make further changes. Larry was asked to leave. That shook him up. He is, by self-description, a simple man with simple goals. He wanted his work, in some manner, to matter, to be connected with eternal realities, to demonstrate the reality of God, to make a difference. He had entered "the ministry" with the idea of investing his life into the lives of others, planting seeds of the Good News in empty hearts. Now—and this is what *really* rocked his world—he would have to give up such lofty desires for work. He would have to take "a job."

His work, he believed, was about to be reduced to mere labor to satisfy a hungry bank account. Work would be a way to provide for his family, to survive, with the necessary implication that living—*real life*—would exist outside the boundaries of his job. He had never given much thought to a theology of work, but he knew enough about the bills spilling from the table that God intended him to pay them.

So he took a job as a medical equipment salesman. His wares: orthopedic supplies.

By the grace of God, the job in many ways seemed to "fit" Larry. He always had the gift for small talk, and a salesman banks on his words. He was pleased when, standing in operating rooms, he saw that the products he was selling provided an invaluable service, reducing the complexities and pain of surgery. He was deeply impressed by men who, seeing his potential, began to invest themselves in his development.

His first surprise: The work, by itself, had inherent value.

In the first few years of the job, Larry was simply trying to get by with his faith intact, to keep his soul from catching in a company shredder. His actions were mostly defensive, protective. He was doing nothing heroic, he says. Then came his second surprise: The work, by itself, gave him a platform to share his faith. After he had proved himself professionally to one surgeon, he was able to build a bridge into the surgeon's private world. Larry began to ask him questions about his wife and his kids, his values, his goals. At first, the doctor didn't welcome such topics of conversation. But over time, they got into discussion of religion versus relationship. Larry had an opportunity to share how Christ had made an impact on the way he treated his wife, the way he raised his kids, the way he did his business.

There were other such conversations with colleagues. His customers—mostly busy doctors—began to take the time to praise him for his commitment to service, his level of knowledge, and his skill. His business associates, although often drunkenly razzing him on the road, began to seek him out when a problem hit home. Increasingly, the questions posed to him had this common theme: "Why? Why don't you go out and get drunk or nudge a few numbers or take that promotion or bad-mouth the boss?"

An even bigger surprise: Larry Watkins—a simple, common man—stood apart.

Once, while on the back nine of a golf course, he was teeing up with a potential customer. "Say," the doctor said after a nearly criminal slice with a three-iron, "what is it with you, anyway? Are you *religious* or something?"

As they casually strolled the fairway, Larry responded with a smile, "My religion is bass fishing; my relationship is with Jesus." With a history of integrity and skill as well as a gift for casual conversation, he had cast a line and was trolling for more—and deeper—questions.

He got them. And he answered them.

Even his manager started to notice. The topic: "You seem to be a devoted family man. How do you balance your career and your family?" So Larry told him. Then he took the bigger opportunity. "Say, at one of our next regional meetings, if you'd like me to, why don't I spend about forty-five minutes with whoever wants to come talking on this area of balancing career and family?"

His boss looked interested.

"But I'd want to be able to use Bible content," Larry added quickly.

"Hmmm. Let me think it over," his boss said. A few days later, the boss called back, "Yeah, why don't you do that at our next meeting? We'll just schedule it before our real meeting begins and make it a voluntary thing for whoever is interested. How does that sound?"

Larry grabbed the opportunity—and a couple of buddies, guys he knew to be borderline believers but not strong in taking a stand among a group.

"Are you sure you want to do this?" one of the friends asked him. "People can get a little rough with their teasing."

"Sure. It's a great platform. It's the reason I work anyway. This job is a mask for what I'm called to do—facilitate the gospel. So are you guys with me?"

"Yeah, I guess so," they said, although a bit reluctantly.

"Good. If it just turns out to be the three of us, that'll be okay, too." So they headed off to Kansas City to the regional meeting. At the end of the first day of meetings with the thirty salespeople, the manager turned to Larry. "So you want to make your announcement now?"

Larry stood up. "Tomorrow morning, we're going to talk about how to work a 24/7 job and still try to maintain a family. So whoever would like to show up, show up. But I need to let you know that it's going to be biblically based. So if that's going to bother you, you probably want to miss it."

Over dinner, Larry's two buddies grew edgy. "Are you sure about this? Do you really think this is the forum to talk about the Bible?"

"Sure it is. What better opportunity?"

Several of the others around the three began to tune into their conversation. As the wine flowed and the dinner came, one of the eavesdroppers called to him from the other end of the dinner table, "Hey, Watkins, you really think that stuff's going to make an impact or a difference? Does church stuff make a difference to you?"

"Sure. And you know what? Not only in me, but in those two guys right there." He pointed to his buddies and silently prayed that they wouldn't bail out on him. They made the right choice and chimed in.

The next morning, all thirty salespeople showed up for the biblically based session on balance. It proved to be a strong meeting. Larry finally understood about evangelism—that it took place most often in a certain context. God had not called him to be a preacher at work. For a time God had called him to be a preacher at a church. He did that. Then God called him to another, different task.

The family member has a mission. The church member has a mission. The worker has a mission. Larry understood that God had not asked him to buttonhole people and preach at them at work. His first call was to be a model worker: to display skill, to serve those around him. He understood that to make a difference he had to work "as unto the Lord" and live his life in a way to earn credibility. In doing so, he slowly and competently built a platform that others readily gathered around.

But then came Larry's fourth surprise: The work, by itself, held potential dangers, traps of the soul.

We saw earlier his conflict with his boss. Coming out of the professional ministry into the medical industry and competing with people who'd networked the industry for years proved tough. The pressure to blend in, to compromise, to be "one of the guys" was strong. Larry recalls one particular evening when the group invited him along to dinner. When an attractive woman seated them, the group began to tease her. They ogled, they commented, they joked. They laughed.

How to respond? When to laugh? When not to laugh? Larry felt as though he were back in junior high, fighting to be part of the gang but not step over the line. When the evening ended and he walked back to the car with his buddies, one of them turned to him and said, "Well, the message you sent back there didn't sound like the one you used last month in Kansas City."

Larry felt stripped to the bone. He sat in stunned, defeated, deafening silence for the ride back to the hotel.

There were other traps along the way. On the road, colleagues would invite him to go out for a few beers at a local strip joint. "Come on," came the line, "your wife will never know." He would say no, of course, and find himself in a hotel room with the cardboard advertisement for adult movies on top of the television, his mind whispering, "Come on, no one will ever know." There was, in fact, an endless stream of "little" temptations—to doctor a company report, pad a bill, blow off a conference meeting, scrap service for competence and excellence for efficiency. He continually sought to define what it meant to "get ahead." When faced with a promotion that would have greatly increased his pay as well as his work hours, he turned it down because of how it might affect his family.

But there was one central theme to his life now—one he would never have experienced as a youth pastor. He was in the fray. He stood dead-center in the high-traffic lane. He had a platform, and he wielded influence. He had a strategy: a work theology that dictated his work standards and defined his personal behavior.

An Intimate Calling

Under the overarching design of stewardship, each person has a calling to work. Like Larry Watkins, you may discover your individual calling quite accidentally, or, like many others, you may search diligently and still find your calling elusive. Because calling is so highly unique—as unique as each individual—no seven-step programs exist for its accurate calculation. Only a heart for God will provide the necessary discernment.

Calling, like stewardship, is critical, and we'll talk more about pursuing it in a later chapter. For now it is enough to know that calling depends upon how a person "sees" work; that is, whether he has a correct theology of work. A person who understands work as a curse from God, an ordeal to be endured, is unlikely to feel "called" to such a gruesome task. On the other hand, if he understands work as a vital, unique, and powerful dimension of abundant living and opportunity for ministry and maturation, then the discovery of a specific calling to work will serve as a major piece in each person's puzzle of purpose.

A calling, above all, originates in God as Creator and his profound and perfect design for each person—in gifts, talents, temperament, passion, and experience. The Father, in this case, truly does know best. Calling is inherently relational, charged with intimacy.

Without an individual calling, exercised under the principle of stewardship, a person will find it impossible to fully realize God's interrelated purposes for work, which are at least fivefold: provision, service, character development, worship, and modeling. These are the answers the Father gives us when we sit at his feet and ask, "Daddy, why should I work?"

1. *Provision.* Work provides the necessities of physical life: food, drink, clothing, and shelter. The Bible, especially in the wisdom literature and Pauline theology, is pregnant with warnings against idleness and exhortations to live productively. (See Prov. 6:6–11, 10:4–5, 10:26, 12:24, 12:27, 13:4, 14:23, 15:19, 18:9, 19:15, 19:24, 20:4, 20:13, 21:25–26, 23:21, 24:30–34, 26:14–16; Eccl. 4:5, 10:18; Isa. 56:10; 1 Tim. 5:13.) Paul is blunt and to the point: "If a man will not work, he shall not eat" (2 Thess. 3:10; see also verses 11–12). Any individual capable of work should do it. Whether paid or voluntary, at home or in the Oval Office, work is not an option.

Work as provision has a communal, as well as individual, purpose. Through the work of men and women, God intends to meet the needs of the poor and the weak. This is a consistent message throughout the Bible. Paul writes, "If anyone does not provide for his relatives, and especially for his immediate family, he has denied the faith and is worse than an unbeliever" (1 Tim. 5:8).

As with all the purposes of work, stewardship is the fuel for provision. If we are charged with the care of God's resources, what is a more precious and vital resource than the people who bear his image?

2. *Service to Others.* Intertwined with the idea of provision is the element of service. Work, as God intended it, always involves a mindset of service to others. In the book of Philippians, Paul exhorts followers of Christ to "do nothing out of selfish ambition or vain conceit, but in humility consider others better than yourselves. Each of you should look not only to your own interests, but also to the interests of others. Your attitude should be the same as that of Christ Jesus" (Phil. 2:3–5). In the verses that follow, speaking of the violence of Christ's transition from God at the center of cosmic worship to a crucified man in the pit of hell, Paul powerfully outlines the central qualities of Jesus' attitude: meekness, commitment, servanthood, humility, obedience, and joy.

In a sense, provision might be defined as one of the acts from a mind focused on service, in much the same way as a widow's split wood results from the act of someone's ax. In today's highly competitive marketplace, it is rare (but less so all the time) to find a business focused on service. We still are hung over from an era of corporate greed when work served mostly as a means to an end: to power, material acquisition, self-esteem, and weekends in southern France.

Viewed through the perspective of stewardship, the mindset of service is what gives work much of its intrinsic value. Peter Drucker states, "The honest work of yesterday has lost its social status, its social esteem."[3] There was a time in our culture when a display of a good strong work ethic clinched a job. "Joe's a fine employee. He really knows how to put in a good day's work." Today, that trait is not enough to win admiration—or a job. We demand brilliance, or ingenious creativity, or great contacts, or diverse experience. Stewardship argues for a return to the intrinsic, productive values of work in the spirit and motivation of servanthood.

Work is designed as both grand and mysterious. We have the opportunity, through simple acts motivated by a spirit of service, to participate with God in the day-to-day spinning of his world. In this sense, the plumber, the preacher, the policeman, and the pool keeper all stand on level ground. Whether he or she unclogs drains or souls or streets or filters, each person contributes to the world through that act a necessary good.

We have the opportunity, through simple acts motivated by a spirit of service, to participate with God in the day-to-day spinning of his world. In this sense, the plumber, the preacher, the policeman, and the pool keeper all stand on level ground.

This utilitarian component of work has nothing to do with "me and my needs." We are supposed to be part of that big machine in life. Our work somehow makes the world a better place. At the end of the day, if it's all about money, then we've left something out: primarily a service to humanity.

3. *Character Development.* By his own admission, Larry Watkins was not a confident man. He struggled to find his place in the world, to define and develop his strengths, to acknowledge and compensate for his weaknesses, and to feel that what he was doing really mattered. His question, asked mostly in whispered 3:00 A.M. prayers, was the same as millions of others: *How can an average guy make an eternal difference?*

That is what drew him to "the ministry." As a youth pastor, he had the opportunity to directly impact the course of eternal reality with every conversion and subsequent spiritual development. Looking back, he says today, his accomplishments came with varying degrees of success. Sometimes, his own sin got in the way. Sometimes, church leaders inadvertently blocked his paths. Sometimes, his own persistent and nagging lack of confidence paralyzed his efforts.

When Larry took a job as a medical salesman, he believed that most of his "ministry" was over. Work would pay the bills. Yet, as we already have seen, Larry Watkins soon discovered a whole new vista—a previously unknown frontier—for displaying the character, words, and acts of God. He did so imperfectly, for sure, and sometimes he even completely and miserably failed. But gradually, with growing confidence, Larry began to have an impact. It was not exactly evangelism, as he had been taught it in most systematic theology, but some people were being drawn to Larry Watkins, "average" guy.

Larry attributes his effectiveness to "the crucible of work." His faith was on the line. As he waited in that doctor's office, just before his first sales pitch, praying that God would help him pay his ever-mounting bills, he made the first of many realizations of his complete dependence on God. If he were to simply survive in the business world with its focus on the strongest, he would have to develop a whole new level of trust. His faith was not only on the line, but was hanging by a thread in a typhoon.

His temptations to fudge his character came early—in his new boss's request to overstock the hospital—and often. A barrage of "opportunities" presented themselves for compromise, manipulation, and self-pursuit: "Do this and you'll get ahead. Go here and you'll see what I'm talking about. Take that and you'll have the edge."

Yet Larry, firm in his desire to serve and growing in his grasp of a work theology, always attempted to take the high path: honesty, excellence, and integrity. He has not always succeeded, but even his failures—and maybe *especially* his failures—contributed to the development of his character. In the crucible of the business world—with its amoral worship of "whatever works"—Larry began to remove the moral sludge from his life. He understood in vivid terms the meaning of Peter's admonishment:

> Make every effort to add to your faith goodness; and to goodness, knowledge; and to knowledge, self-control; and to self-control, perseverance; and to perseverance, godliness; and to godliness, brotherly

kindness; and to brotherly kindness, love. For if you possess these qualities in increasing measure, they will keep you from being ineffective and unproductive in your knowledge of our Lord Jesus Christ. (2 Peter 1:5–8)

These words were no longer simply ink on paper, but essential nourishment for his soul's survival.

As Larry sought to stay true to his theological compass and clock, his anchors in time and space, a curious thing happened to him. For the first time in his life, he had a sense of his own competence, which was remarkably free of ego. In the specific calling of his job—which he did not even recognize—God allowed him to exercise not only his faith, but his own unique gifts, temperament, talents, and passions. In other words, God was maturing Larry Watkins. He was no longer Larry Watkins, the average guy, but Larry Watkins, the incredibly unique and loving creation of God.

4. *Worship.* Scripture also has much to say about worship. Over and over we are told what should be worshiped (God) and what should not be worshiped (anything other than God), to the point that we might think God's being rather redundant if it weren't for the fact that we so frequently disobey his repeated command.

And where should we worship God? A quick tour of Scripture provides a partial list: on the mountain, in the desert, in Hebron, at his sanctuary, on the Mount of Olives, in bed, in the Temple, on the battlefields, in the heavens, in front of gates, in Jerusalem, in Judah, in Babylon, in a manger in Bethlehem, at feasts, and at the feet of angels. In short, we should worship God wherever God happens to be—which is everywhere.

But it's more than the physical. As Jesus put it, "Yet a time is coming and has now come when the true worshipers will worship the Father in spirit and truth, for they are the kind of worshipers the Father seeks. God is spirit, and his worshipers must worship in spirit and in truth" (John 4:23–24).

When the Bible talks about working as unto the Lord (Col. 3:23), it's talking about an intimate relationship that is born in and resides in both spirit and in truth. The quest, then, is not for a public display of worship to God, but a genuine search for a relationship that comes from worshiping the Creator and Redeemer in every possible way and in every possible place.

We worship the Lord when we sit among our friends and sing praises during a church service. So, too, can we worship the Lord when we dance alone on a moonlit beach. Or when we hike through unexplored forests. Or when we welcome the morning sun with a cup of coffee in one hand and a fishing rod in the other.

Or when we work. It's not so much where we are or what we're doing as much as for whom we are doing it. Our work, if it is done unto the Lord, is pleasing to God, is an intimate expression of our love for him and our desire to embrace a vertical relationship with truth and life. It goes all the way back to Genesis, where God did the work and proclaimed it good. A job well done glorifies God, regardless of whether anyone else knows about it.

Nowhere, perhaps, is our call to worship God in all spheres of life more clearly given than in the poetry of the Psalms, and, in particular, in the eleven verses of the Psalm 63:

> O God, you are my God,
> > earnestly I seek you;
> my soul thirsts for you,
> > my body longs for you,
> in a dry and weary land
> > where there is no water.
> I have seen you in the sanctuary
> > and beheld your power and your glory.
> Because your love is better than life,
> > my lips will glorify you.
> I will praise you as long as I live,
> > and in your name I will lift up my hands.
> My soul will be satisfied
> > as with the richest of foods;
> with singing lips
> > my mouth will praise you.
> On my bed I remember you;
> > I think of you
> > through the watches of the night.
> Because you are my help,
> > I sing in the shadow of your wings.
> My soul clings to you;
> > your right hand upholds me.

They who seek my life
  will be destroyed;
they will go down
  to the depths of the earth.
They will be given over to the sword
  and become food for jackals.
But the king will rejoice in God;
  all who swear by God's name will praise him,
while the mouths of liars will be silenced.

5. *Modeling.* But worship through our work doesn't always center on what we *do.* Worship can be the result of who we *are.* Worship is a reflection of God's character from our lives. The core definition of worship is to ascribe value and worth to God. Worship involves a pause on our part: We look at God and ascribe value to him for who he is. Our lives, a living sacrifice, can initiate an act of worship for others. They look at our lives, our God-given skills, our blessings, and ascribe value to God. We reflect him, causing others to worship him.

Consider the way we use the word *work*: A small child, when her toy is broken, comes to her father or mother and says, "It doesn't work." What a curious thing to say. Wouldn't "it doesn't *play*" be much more accurate? Yet nine times out of ten the common response to brokenness, by adult or child, is to say without thinking, "It doesn't *work.*" Our choice of vocabulary is profound, revealing. It springs from a deep reality of the cosmos: Things are supposed to work. And by *work* we intrinsically mean *work correctly*, according to their design, function, and purpose.

> But worship through our work doesn't always center on what we *do.* Worship can be the result of who we *are.* Worship is a reflection of God's character from our lives.

Boats, with their slicing blue-white wakes, are exquisite and graceful in water. Airplanes, trailing comets on a canvas sky, are truly things of beauty. And is there anything lovelier than a silver maple in spring, its new leaves dancing in morning light? But what happens when you put a boat in the desert, a plane under water, or a tree in a fire? It doesn't work, either functionally or—more curiously—aesthetically. A thing of great beauty is transformed into an intuitively ugly reality. Still again, have you ever caught yourself saying, "It just doesn't work for me"? What do you mean? What are you really saying?

Work is supposed to work. And in a very deep sense, Jesus *worked*, double entendre intended. His work involved modeling the life, character, words, and actions of God. In John 5:19, Jesus explained, "I tell you the truth, the Son can do nothing by himself; he can do only what he sees his Father doing, because whatever the Father does the Son also does."

In Jesus' words reside many great realities, but not the least of which is this: man—the perfect, sinless man; man as God intended and designed man to be—truly and naturally models God just as water reflects light, a river returns to the sea, and leaves whisper in the wind. The creature can't help resembling the Creator.

The Fall, however, produced an overwhelming sense of cosmic brokenness, releasing a terrifying chaos in the natural order of reality. Disruption, sin, and death now reign in the place previously occupied by worship. The man who seeks after God first comes to this terrible and painful realization: "Daddy, my soul doesn't work."

It is not surprising, then, that the work of fallen man simply doesn't work. Blinded by selfish ambition, stripped of worship, maimed by greed and lust, stunted by sin, he resembles a tiny, crippled, naked beggar who, in the words of C. S. Lewis, is apt to mistake jumping in a mud puddle for a luxury cruise on the sea. Most of the time, he models little more than his own puny self.

Yet even in fallen humanity, worship can be expressed through work. Michael Jordan starts from the foul line, twisting and arching his body, and ends with a reverse slam: pure grace. Or Bill Gates, focused and ambitious, types the program to another seamless application: the ability to bring order to what was complex. Their skill showcases the undeniable evidence of a Creator. A new mother, single and alone and exhausted, wraps her arms around her sick and crying baby: selfless love—evidence of a Creator. A surgeon, with steady hands and beads of sweat on her brow, carefully replaces a failing lung with one from another human being: indisputable skill, and evidence of a Creator.

To be created in the image of God, broken as it is now by sin, means that life sometimes works as it is supposed to, regardless. In our mostly tragic world, there are still natural reflections—dim yet powerful—of God. Evidence spills out of the work environment that there is something going on that is bigger than all of us and that there is a real, approachable God.

But the power of sin is great. It draws us to the mirror, not the Maker. It reduces, fragments, separates, and corrupts. It leaves us to our own weak self, and our work—in direct proportion to our isolation—naturally turns mean. We become consumed by the need to achieve, get, earn, accumulate, and hoard. Without the transforming and re-creating work of God, it is impossible to connect our work to its intended purposes, to operate under a correct work theology. Just as Jesus learned to model God, followers of Christ must learn from the Son. "I am the vine; you are the branches," Jesus said in John 15:5. "If a man remains in me and I in him, he will bear much fruit; apart from me you can do nothing."

We can best reflect God on the job by:

- Displaying purity.
- Building strong relationships.
- Focusing on the task at hand.
- Showing mercy and compassion at work.
- Providing servant leadership.
- Managing time well.
- Offering counsel to the confused.
- Demonstrating balance.
- Offering forgiveness in conflict.
- Setting correct priorities.
- Expressing the God-viewpoint on issues in the workplace.

In short, we model Christ in the marketplace in four categorical ways: evidence his calling; display character; deliver skill; serve others.

Only as we learn of the life and character of Jesus can we begin to reflect his words and deeds in our own work. To model him. To do his work. And slowly, he re-creates us into the people we were originally created to be: fully human, uniquely gifted, natural in worship, and tirelessly productive. Our work begins to work. As a light does in a dark place.

PART II

INTEGRATING A VERY FRAGMENTED LIFE

LAUNCHING PADS:
REMEMBERING EARLY PIONEERS

ON THE SOUTHWESTERN tip of the continent of Europe, marking a borderland to a vast watery unknown, was a village on what had been christened "the Sacred Promontory." During the fifteenth century, in the country of Portugal, it was called Sagres. From this hamlet, the whole world was changed.

The prominent view from Sagres was the limitless expanse of potential, encouraged by circumstance, and fueled by imagination. Unlike most European countries, Portugal was not distracted by dogma or commerce. Its eventual mission, modern exploration, was at first more a result of what it lacked: a heartfelt bigotry (which fueled the raging of religious wars) and a Mediterranean seaport (which prevented it from a lucrative sea trade). It was a cosmopolitan country in search of a singular vision to which it could give its undistracted attention.

Along came Prince Henry the Navigator. Henry was the third son of King John I, known as either the Great or the Bastard, who had seized the Portuguese throne in 1385. In many ways, Henry was a living paradox: the father of modern exploration, he was himself a homebody. Continually pregnant with vision and far-reaching in mind, he was believed to have lived like a hermit and died a virgin. Yet, his contribution to discoveries was critical. Writes Daniel Boorstin, "Modern exploration had to be an adventure of the mind, a thrust of someone's imagination, before it became a worldwide adventure of seafaring."[1]

Prince Henry was a master of integration. Much like a modern research-and-development company, Henry systematically, powerfully, and intuitively brought together the past and the present, what already was and what could be, and launched the world into its greatest era of discovery.

Because most of the world's current maps were wildly inaccurate—reflecting the misled theology of Christian geographers—Henry meticulously began accumulating information from previous and present explorers. Cartography, for the first time in history, became a cumulative science. Boorstin writes that Henry "knew that the unknown could only be discovered by clearly marking the boundaries of the known."[2]

Henry did the same with navigation and shipbuilding. Fearlessly coupling technology with current models, he focused on a pragmatic question: What will allow us to go further? The compass was freed from its superstitious cages. The cross-staff, a graduated stick that helped define latitude, was invented. New mathematical tables were written.

In shipbuilding, Henry quickly discovered that the dominant design—the heavy, square-rigged barca used in the Mediterranean Sea trade—was woefully inadequate for exploring. Such ships were almost impossible to sail against the wind, far too heavy, and inherently clumsy. They lacked maneuverability and flexibility.

Henry brought together engineers and shipbuilders. Together, they studied alternative models: the ancient Arabic caravos, modeled on the even more ancient Greek fishing vessels. Rigged with slanting and triangular sails, the ships were designed to carry Arab crews of about thirty, as well as about seventy horses—a much smaller cargo than the bulky Mediterranean ships. Also in use was the even smaller, more maneuverable caravela on a northern Portuguese river. From these present designs sprung the hybrid—the caravel—a ship combining the cargo-carrying features of the caravos with the greater maneuverability of the caravela. The caravel would soon become the standard ship for discovery.

Since the primary commerce of modern exploration was ideas, the necessary cargo was the return of the sailors with newly discovered concepts. In the wise implementation of technology applied toward a vision, the present and the past bred an entirely new future. Henry's genius was the ever-reaching adventure of his mind.

Find and Follow a Great Model

We as authors have drawn much of what we do from watching others do it well. Growing up, I (Steve) always watched and measured the work ethic of vocational ministers against that of my mom. She was the hardest worker I've ever known. She never uttered the familiar excuse, "Life isn't fair."

Let me explain. For the first twelve years of my life, Mom was a stay-at-home worker who took extra part-time jobs to make ends meet. My dad took his orders from the Air Force. At that age, I never totally understood the Air Force situation; I just knew it took my dad away for months and years at a time. Somewhere between the third and seventh grades, I realized that my dad wasn't going to be living with us often. So from seventh grade on, I grew up with a mom who worked at least two jobs all the time. She worked as a church secretary, signed on as an administrative assistant, ran a Hallmark gift shop, clerked at Dillard's. Like many other women of that era, she had grown up without a formal education, married, and then coped with what life dealt her. She had no résumé. She had no track record. She had no diploma. But she had no complaints.

And she always found a job. If it didn't work out, Mom found another one. A godly woman, she built a Christian home and set the pattern and principles of work in my life.

Following her model, I also contributed to the family income. I worked after school, on the weekends, in the summer. I bought my own clothes, my car, all the extras. Basically, I figured out what jobs would fit around my sports and school schedules. And through those junior high and high school years, I began to think about what I wanted to do long term. First, I toyed with the idea of a career in the fish-and-game world. The adventure stories I read had planted dreams of various jobs around the world connected to the outdoors.

Then for a time I decided I wanted to go into law, maybe to become a supreme court justice. You know—ride in the limousines and wear the black robes. I was argumentative (ask Tom), confrontational, direct, verbal, and analytical. Watching Perry Mason on TV, I'd walk away saying, "I can do that job. I could take somebody to the hoop on that issue."

But toward the end of high school, I fell into step with David Rogers, an incredible coach who'd had a dramatic conversion and had become a part-time youth pastor at our church. I began to wrestle with the whole issue of what it meant to have a life-consuming passion for Christ. What did that look like? Could it be a reality? Could you make a living working in jobs you loved and still be sold out to God?

I headed off to college and seminary to major in theology and Greek. My goal wasn't to become a vocational minister, but to learn the Bible and to develop a deep understanding of truth that would benefit me in any work assignment that came along. Instead of pastoring a church on the weekends, as some of my buddies did, I kept my foot in the business community. To get rich was never the goal; to walk with Jesus was my passion.

As I studied the curriculum, I also studied people. Because I liked the tag-team approach to learning, I'd read a book and then look for a living, breathing model. Then I went back to the books to validate and put a context around what I'd observed. I became a sponge around people living the abundant life. Manly Beasley, an itinerant Bible preacher, was one of those guys, a real mystic with the gift of faith. I dropped out of college to be around him for a year. Supporting dozens of missionaries around the world, he never had a marketing plan. Instead he trusted God. He'd say things like, "God told me that we'll have lunch here about 11:45, so let's just work until then." And sure enough, about 11:45, somebody would show up at his office with Subway sandwiches. I'd look at him and think, *What's the deal?* I could hardly fathom the intimate relationship he had with God. After two years of academic study of the Bible, a year with Manly proved to be the perfect laboratory.

After finishing my degree, I began to work in areas of ministry that overlapped with business—teaching Bible-training seminars, speaking to men's groups, serving as an executive coach to business leaders. The long and short of it: My entire early life history pointed to The Life@Work Co., how to live out who you are in the marketplace, with the gifts God has given you, to change the world for Christ.

Tom's personal journey led him to the same destination.

Purpose and Progress

I (Tom) can define my parents in two words: *purpose* and *progress*. To the extent that life can be figured out, my parents definitely were figure-it-out kind of people. They grew. They learned. They embraced productivity. They accomplished. But money never entered the discussion. As a medical doctor, my dad had opportunities to climb to the top rung of his career ladder, but that was never his goal. Progress and accomplishment meant something different to my parents; they were tied to an all-consuming purpose. It was a distinction that colors my thinking to this day.

To my parents, progress meant you had to accomplish something, to learn something. Progress meant you'd better not be the same person you were a year ago. Progress meant you had to know where you were going and you actually had to get there. Purpose, on the other hand, was a transcendent cause that God placed on your heart for you to live out.

My dad came out of college and the Navy during World War II with a civil engineering degree. Then he and Mom worked for InterVarsity Christian Fellowship, an international ministry to college students. As newlyweds they moved across the country to attend seminary. Then they applied for candidacy to the Evangelical Free Church Mission Board for overseas missions. As part of the interviewing process, my dad asked them what kind of missionaries the organization needed. "Doctors," the board responded. So my dad decided to go to medical school.

When he finished medical school, he and Mom moved to Hong Kong, with all five of us kids in tow. I had no idea what "Communist China" really was, but from my parents' tone, I gathered it was a fearful thing.

Once there, my dad teamed up with his partner, Dr. Bob Chapman, to set up an outpatient practice at a local mission. Within a year, it became clear that the larger need was for a hospital, and Dr. Chapman and my dad agreed to take on the project of establishing one.

At first my dad resisted the idea. He had no money and no experience with that kind of work. Besides, the logistical obstacles would be a nightmare. But the British government, who had asked Dad to build the hospital, wouldn't take no for an answer, so Dad agreed to reconsider it. And the project soon became central to fulfilling his purpose and progress as a missionary doctor.

The upshot: my dad and his partner built and dedicated a new hospital near the airport, debt-free. As superintendent of the hospital, Dad was the liaison with the architect, he was the engineer involved, he repaired the boiler when it didn't work. Rather than the typical four-year stint overseas, we stayed five so he could complete the project.

But the hospital didn't have a surgeon, so when we came home on leave, Dad began a surgical residency for two years. Purpose and progress. His mindset: you plan where you're going, and then you get there.

We returned to Hong Kong. My brother and I each took summer jobs for a dollar an hour in Hong Kong currency—seventeen cents an hour in American money. Our job was to go room to room in the hospital and scrape off all the whitewash. First, you had to wet it down. Then scrape it off. Then patch up the banged-up walls. Then sand them down. Then paint the ceiling with whitewash again. Then brush on two coats of oil-based paint. There was no air-conditioning. It was hot, messy, and we were making almost nothing. We worked five days a week, all day long, with a twenty-minute break in the morning and afternoon and a half-hour for lunch.

Lunch became the issue that instigated my first labor strike. The hospital administrator, a part-time missionary, decided to cut costs. So he informed us that we would get no more free lunches. From the next day forward, he told us, our Chinese lunch would cost us one dollar. We didn't show up the next day. "If you can find somebody else," we told him, "who will work as cheaply as we do, go ahead." After our one-day strike, we reported for work the following day and got our free lunch again.

But I was getting smarter. For the next job, I invested my earnings in an old manual typewriter and opted for typing up the doctors' dictation. I later became a full-fledged surgery assistant to my dad. Not just his scrubber, mind you, but his real assistant, holding his vac tubes and providing his instruments. But after a few surgeries, even that job proved to be long, boring, tedious, and messy. If I looked away from the wound during those four-, five-, or eight-hour surgeries and his retractor got misplaced, his reprimand was quick: "Either stay with me, or get out."

> Why are you in the job you have? What are your expectations about work? How God-connected do you believe your work is? Do you feel a sense of calling to your job? The answers to these questions may be the root of your purpose and peace of mind in the marketplace.

So where did that personal journey lead me? I grew up assuming work was going to be difficult and that the pay wasn't going to be good. Work called for plans, preparation, persistence, patience, and progress—all for a purpose.

When Steve and I met, I was teaching at the University of Arkansas and consulting part-time with some local companies. Steve was leading a ministry aimed primarily at business leaders. We quickly recognized that we shared a passion both for God and for the marketplace, and we soon cofounded a consulting firm, Cornerstone Group, based on the idea of blending biblical principles and business excellence. A few years later, The Life@Work Co. was launched to take that message to a broader audience through such vehicles as books, conferences, and *The Life@Work Journal*.

Why give our personal stories here in this discussion of work history? To encourage you to reflect on your own work history. Why are you in the job you have? What are your expectations about work? How God-connected do you believe your work is? Do you feel a sense of calling to your job? The answers to these questions may be the root of your purpose and peace of mind in the marketplace.

Viewing the Present Through the Lens of the Past

G. K. Chesterton once wrote that history is the hill we stand upon to see the town in which we live. The implication: Without knowledge of the past, the present is unknowable. As individuals we have a history. And that history often explains our present.

This is certainly true for our nation. Our history explains our present marketplace pressure, pace, and potential. Likewise, an exploration of the Fourth Frontier is more a return than a discovery—it is a rediscovery of our cultural roots. How did we ever get to the place where we thought that to be good Christians we had to quit our jobs and become full-time "ministers," sail for foreign shores to serve as a missionary, or run a homeless shelter? All those assignments are good. But those jobs have no higher value than any other assignment God gives to his people. And he gives many and varied assignments to his people.

History is not a loose and windblown collection of dry facts and dates, but a sturdy suitcase passed down through the generations: packed with tattered maps, dog-eared journals, and half-forgotten dreams. Heritage, if nothing else, whispers to us that we are never fully strangers.

Birthed in the earthy spirituality of the Reformers, nursed on the tenacity of opportunity, and often weaned on greed, there is no stronger link in the chain of this country's development—for good or bad—than the ethic of hard work. In fact, on the subject of work, it is difficult to separate the words of the preacher Cotton Mather from those of the pragmatist Ben Franklin. In school, we teethed on Franklin's pragmatic decision-making lists of pros and cons. In *Poor Richard's Almanac* (1757), he insisted, "God helps them that help themselves." And Mather agreed: "Our opportunities to do good are our talents."

The recent refocus on "core competencies" by corporations and the "competency assessments" for individual employees that human resources departments have been circulating for the past five years are not new ideas. From our heritage, both personal and as a nation, we learned that work is inherently good, a source of blessing, and ennobling. Understanding these underlying beliefs is critical to discerning the evolution of work in this country. Work, driven by a catalyst of new technology, may veer from foundational principles of dignity and benefit, but never permanently. In fact, in many critical ways, the shift in work values occurring over the last seven decades in this country—and especially in the last few years—represents a return of the pendulum to the original, foundational ideas of work.

Although history is fluid, some general periods, bookmarked by technological turning points, can be identified.

PERIOD	DRIVING FORCE
The sacred/secular split (300 to 1517)	The Early Church
The sacred/secular healing (1517 to 1730)	The Reformation
The fragmentation of work (1730 to late 1900s)	The Industrial Revolution
The integration of work (late 1900s forward)	The New Economy

Note that in the first two eras, the church took work apart and then put it back together again, while in the second two eras, culture took work apart and now is putting it back together again. We will explore each of these periods in detail but for now, understand that today's hunger for wholeness is being driven by culture, not the church.

Recently we were invited to speak at the Ford company to a group of engineers from the United States, the United Kingdom, and Europe. For these tough, knowledgeable, hard-side-of-the-business engineers, we were asked to speak on calling, serving, character, and skill. Not only was the requested topic unusual, the response was phenomenal. Engineer after engineer asked questions like these: "How do you ever know what your calling is?" "What kind of process can you go through to figure out your calling?" "Have you ever known anybody who quit a job and made a total career change?" The irony of this public-company venue and secular audience was this: Identifying one's calling is a specifically Christian process. Through the Scripture, Jesus calls us individually. This group desperately wanted what they'd never experience outside of Christ.

As the world enters another millennium, we're crossing over into a new era of work culture. Still colored by history's original assumptions, we're rediscovering what work means to us. In much the same way that smoke from a volcano signifies seismic and chemical activity, every critical indication points to dramatic change. First, there is the rise of a powerful new technology—telecommunications. Second, the resurgence of spirituality signifies an increasing cultural desire for a more holistic lifestyle. And third, people are everywhere searching for meaning beyond the static definitions of money.

All three of these interconnected realities are greatly changing the way we work. And many of the changes are in fact driven by what propelled work centuries ago: the demand for dignity, purpose, and connections to transcendent ideas.

To understand the village (global or otherwise) where we now live, we must climb the hill of history. No other perspective will give us a clearer picture. Let's revisit some of the pioneers and evaluate their lasting legacies.

Rebels with a Cause

The Sacred/Secular Split and Healing

When Martin Luther nailed his famous ninety-five theses on the door of the castle church at Wittenberg, he ignited a fire of sweeping change that we now gently refer to as the Reformation. In the history of Western civilization, little exists that the Reformation did not alter. As followers of Christ, we understand its enormous impact on the direction of the church; the thinking of reformers transformed such critical theological issues as salvation, grace, and the authority of the Bible.

> In the history of Western civilization, little exists that the Reformation did not alter.

But the effects of the Reformation did not stop with the church. The world was dramatically changed; it might be safe to say that, with the exception of its direction and speed of spinning, nothing remained the same on the planet Earth. Nowhere was the change as dramatic and world altering as in the idea of work. Through the Reformation, work was once again tied to religious authority. People began to consider physical work as God-ordained and vitally spiritual. The reformers distrusted the growing distance between the sacred and the secular that the spiritual hierarchy in the Roman Catholic Church drove. At the core of the Reformers' protest was the issue of priesthood.

From the third century forward, a division had existed within the church between the clergy, who performed the function of priests (intercessors between God and man), and the laity, who mostly did all the other work. Over time, the idea of work was severed into mostly unspoken dichotomies:

CLERGY	LAITY
God's Work	Common Work
Spiritual	Physical
Sacred	Profane
Eternal	Temporal

One of the great achievements of the Reformation was to reconnect the physical and the spiritual. In the Reformers' insistence upon the "priest-hood of all believers," they loosened all other related distinctions. By virtue of their baptism into the Christian faith, Luther argued, both laypersons who do "secular" work and priests who do "spiritual" work are of the same "spiritual estate." The work of a blacksmith, then, was every bit as "spiritual" as that of the pope. Any difference in work was a matter of function, not value or significance.

After the Reformation, any difference in work was a matter of function, not value or significance.

The Reformers provided a theological sanction for secular work. Luther and Calvin shared these ideas:

• Work is a means by which we glorify God by fulfilling our calling.
• Work is a means to love God by loving our neighbor.
• Work is a means by which we learn and understand our need for God.
• Work provides for our needs and benefits the community.

Few today would argue with their conclusions.

For the Puritans who inherited these ideas, a particular calling to work intertwined with a general calling to godly living. The value of work, which Puritans held in high esteem, was twofold: outward contentment and inward submission to God.

But the Puritans, anchored in the theology of Luther and Calvin, soon found themselves swept over by a global tide of commerce. Ignited by the technology of machine, the world of work was about to become a very different place.

The Cultural Fragmentation of Work

Before the 1730s, work was mostly a local process: A blacksmith, working in a shop next to his house in a small community, stayed with a task from start to finish. He measured the horse's hooves, fired the kiln, heated the iron, pounded it into shape, cooled the shoes, and nailed them into place. He was a craftsman, using his gifts, intelligence, experience, and tools to complete the job. He took pride in his work. Anchored in the thinking of the Reformers, the blacksmith worked to provide for his family, to serve his community, and to glorify God.

But several forces catalyzed dramatic changes once again: the birth of Enlightenment thinking, the rise of the machine, the publication of *The Wealth of Nations,* and the articulation of the new calling: self-improvement. Enlightenment thinking replaced God as the center of the cosmos with man, and that twist in thinking quite naturally elevated the importance of work.

With the rise of the machine, new technology revolutionized the cotton textile industry in England during the 1730s. The inventions of the flying shuttle, spinning jenny, water frame, and machine loom dramatically increased per capita production. Machines led to the growth of factories. The invention of the steam engine in 1769 accelerated the factory system, providing the necessary power for more modern mechanization. This use of steam power led in turn to increased demand for coal and iron. Each development spawned new technological breakthroughs, as, for example, Sir Henry Bessemer's process for making steel. With each new machine and each new process, other industries such as chemicals, mining, and engineering, developed rapidly.

In 1776, Adam Smith's *Wealth of Nations* married the new technology to a vision. In one of the most influential economic books ever written, Smith argued that a division of labor improves productivity; society benefits when people are allowed to pursue self-interests; competition, if allowed free rein, will regulate prices and wages, producing great social benefits.

At the same time North America, a very young but rising continent exploded with an unparalleled spirit of opportunity. Largely unshackled by the social castes of more developed nations, Americans—nourished on the work ethic of the Reformers—truly believed that *anything* was possible.

> In colonial America, the personal calling was modified by the worldly values of opportunity and self-improvement . . . the American ministerial elite worried that a communitarian and God-centered universe was being undermined by a spirit of self-interest and entrepreneurial drive. Worldly gain through competition became the new justification for hard work.[3]

It was an era buoyant with endless possibility for the new. And America was saturated with the new: country, land, opportunity, calling, frontiers, optimism, and ideas. *Frontier* became more than just a word to describe an unexplored territory; it became a metaphor to drive the country. For the most part, both figuratively and symbolically, the country had no boundaries. Limitations of more established nations, such as social castes, shortage of land, heritage, and genetics were nearly nonexistent. Even God—once at the controlling center—would no longer interfere. Work, still a toil, could lead to—make that *had better lead to*—riches.

Opportunity for wealth, however, always carries with it a certain price. While some achieved wealth through work, many felt alienated. As America became more mechanized, the nature of work again changed dramatically. Once involving the completion of a task from beginning to finish, work now became a series of disconnected and repetitive tasks. Technique replaced craft. Efficiency rooted out creativity. The promise of money replaced purpose. Factories in the city drove out workshops in the small community. Perhaps for the first time in history, outside the devastating realm of slavery, workers were permitted—even encouraged—to be less than human. Work and progress required strong dependable bodies. That was all. Anything else just got in the way.

Workers, disconnected from purpose, eventually began to rebel, especially after it became clear that opportunity, in the end, was the property of just a few. Workers united into unions. Management—a new breed of worker necessary to oversee the disconnected tasks—looked for new ways to motivate bored and alienated workers. Segmentation bred territorialism.

Mass transits filled with disconnected minds. Time clocks and stopwatches began ticking off labor.

By the beginning of the twentieth century, workers had been reduced to the level of Pavlovian dogs. Frederick Taylor, a short-lived management guru, believed that workers could be "scientifically managed," conditioned for certain efficient responses.

Following much tension, slowdowns, strikes, and often violence between workers and management, most people concluded that "scientific management" was a poor method of motivation. The tie between work and "godly" virtue—still foundational in the nation's psyche—had been nearly severed.

Eventually a new breed of analysts emerged to speak what was an obvious truth: In order for work to succeed, companies must be sensitive to the need for human dignity. Social scientists like Kurt Lewin, Abraham Maslov, Douglas McGregor, Frederick Herzberg, and Richard Walton argued for a work environment of openness, communication, and trust, rather than control and punishment.

The Integration of Work

To a greater or lesser extent, the human relations movement reconnected workers with fundamental values: work as process, creative, cooperative, dignified, and valued. In other words, we came full circle back to our Reformation roots.

God, however, was no longer the mover and shaker and source of such necessary change. Profit was. Common sense—not commonwealth—was the Big Dog shepherding transition. The backbone of the Reformation work ethic—moral obligation—was no longer capable of motivating people increasingly accustomed to instant gratification. Business found itself in a tenuous and volatile balance. Economic necessity drove change. The hard side of business purred.

> Each generation in today's workforce packed a different bag and has traveled a different journey. But we've landed at the same place: A call for ethics in business and a chance to grow our spiritual nature.

Total Quality Management, reengineering, partnering, and the like began to drive the philosophical underpinnings of the business machine. About the same time, workers began to demand more from their work. Boomers, nursed on the rebellion of the sixties, demanded involvement and relevance, even if the size of their paycheck just so happened to contribute greatly to such noble ideas. And the work world continued to change. The so-called Gen-Xers, in some ways, have accelerated the demand for dignity in work. Increasingly, shorter "projects" are taking the place of the "career shifts" of boomers. Such projects are judged not by the size of the paycheck, but by their inherent purpose. Each generation in today's workforce packed a different bag and has traveled a different journey. But we've landed at the same place: a call for ethics in business and a chance to grow our spiritual nature.

Where History Has Brought Us

John Tyson, chairman of the board at Tyson Foods and a new believer, is determined to connect these two dots. We speak at Tyson's headquarters every two months, and recently the topic was ethics. I (Steve) was taking questions from the floor when someone fired off this one: "What if your boss tells you to do something wrong or illegal?"

"I think that's my question," John Tyson responded, as he stood to his feet. He turned to face the audience of his publicly held company. "That's not the way we want to do business here."

Company after company in the New Economy has come to the same fork in the road. Good ethics is good business. But it's not just about ethics. A recent headline in the *Arkansas Democrat-Gazette* announced: "Nothing Chicken About It: Tyson Execs Give the OK to Bring Religion into the Workplace."[4]

The voluntary attendance at workshops focusing on spiritual issues doesn't surprise the seminar organizers, considering the changes they've noticed over the past year at the nation's largest poultry processor. The story goes on to outline those changes: Bible study and prayers offered at gatherings before or after work hours; people communicating better, listening to each other; a concern for employees' welfare beyond the job, including hiring chaplains to counsel people going through personal crises.[5]

The results at Tyson reflect those of recent research done by McKinsey & Company, Australia, and reported in *BusinessWeek*. When companies set up programs that use spiritual techniques, employee productivity improves and turnover decreases.[6]

The issue is not having "church" at work; the idea is to connect God to our work.

To illustrate still further where our historical journey has led, consider the work culture at Synovus Financial Corp., whose mission statement and people embrace both the secular and the religious. Synovus is a holding company for a group of financial service businesses, including a network of thirty-eight banking companies. The company carries more than $12 billion in assets and employs more than ten thousand people.

Explains Lee Lee James, who worked her way up through the company during the last fourteen years and is now president of Synovus Service, an arm of the financial holding company, "If we teach people what it's like to be served and what it's like to have someone care about [them], they, in turn, do it for others, and our business gets better. But [they] do it because it's the right thing to do. And that's a good enough end in itself."[7] But you hear it not only from Lee Lee James; these two comments surface quite often in other hallway and conference room conversations: "It's the right thing to do," and "Treat people right."

Does it work? In 1999, *Fortune* magazine declared Synovus the best company to work for in America. And in 1997, Synovus stock ranked ten in the "100 Best Stocks to Own in America."[8]

Believers working together in the marketplace to spread the Good News—we've come full circle.

In a nutshell, here's the history of work from the time of Christ to Chrysler: Soon after the birth of the New Testament church, people began to separate work into the secular and the sacred. That thinking dominated the thinking of the church and permeated culture in most of the known world. The second era began with the Reformation. Martin Luther suggested that work itself was sacred and glorified God, that a person's daily work or calling had eternal significance. That Reformation thinking held sway until the beginning of the Industrial Revolution. The church pulled God and work apart and then put them back together.

In the third era, the culture with the Industrial Revolution began to segment work again to gain efficiency. People became specialists (engineers, electricians, plumbers) rather than generalists (farmers, builders). The Industrial Revolution fragmented work and therefore fragmented life. In the New Economy, people have a hunger for wholeness. There's a tremendous movement to put our work and our soul back together again.

In short, work is closer now than ever to a return to the Reformation motive of making work, well, *work*. As we stand on the precipice of the third millennium, cultural, technological, and historical forces are combining to create another new era of work, one that is neither secular *nor* sacred, but both.

And while this current dramatic change is being driven by the culture rather than by the church, it calls disciples of Christ to join—and influence—the trip.

SHIPWRECKED:
THE FRAGMENTED LIFE

FOR THE LONGEST time, no one dared call it the New World. Christopher Columbus—the first to successfully sail west across the Atlantic—and Amerigo Vespucci, who followed within the decade, merely sought a new route into an already discovered land. Creative and fearless, neither discoverer possessed enough imagination or guts to proclaim a new continent—a fourth part of the world.

In fact, both explorers shared a vested interest in the old terra firma. Operating from the writings of Marco Polo, Columbus and Vespucci believed they could sail west and discover a sea passage through a narrow strait that led to the Indian Ocean. From there, it was on to the "Indies" and "Cinpangu" (Japan)—lands of vast wealth that were lush with gold, spices, cotton, exotic animals, and unimaginable beauty. They sailed under the flag of certain riches. They risked their lives, sailing into unknown waters for a known destination.

For them, the reality of an undiscovered land was an obstacle, and as it turned out, it was nearly as large as the world is long. Columbus was stubborn. On his first voyage, he mistook an aromatic shrub for cinnamon, an inedible nut for a coconut, and the island of Cuba for the continent of Asia. Brilliant and unmatched on the open sea, a master of changing winds, he was on land a slave to the power and inflexibility of his dream.

Vespucci, on the other hand, with his omnivorous curiosity and high intellect, was rational and meticulous. Vespucci searched nearly ten months for the passage into the Indian Ocean by following along nearly 2,400 miles of the South American coastline. Although he provided intricate details of the lives of the natives, he never found what he was really looking for—a sea passage to proven treasure. Still determined, Vespucci returned home, changed flags from

*Portuguese to Spanish, and planned another voyage. This time, he would sail
north and west where before he sailed south—discovery by the process of elimi-
nation. Before he could sail, however, he died of malaria, which he had contracted
on his previous voyage.*

*Both men went to their graves believing they were closer to an old continent—
Asia—than to a new and as yet unnamed frontier. Even for daring and committed explorers, the true nature of discovery never quite falls along the latitudes of
the expected.*

Encountering the Unexpected

Rogers Kirven had arrived at his life's predetermined destination—or so
he believed. With the restless itch and passion of a man born to be an entrepreneur, he had created, built, and nurtured six companies into a thriving
enterprise. His goal always had been the same: to be counted in the top
1 percent of the nation's wealthiest people. In 1997, at the age of forty-four,
he had opportunities to sell his companies, to feed his ego—not to mention
his bank account—with the necessary numbers. He could cash out. His goal
achieved, he then could move on to less pressing but entirely desirable matters: more time with his family, his faith, and personal discovery—not to
mention his toys. And no more work.

In his relentlessly rational mind, this decision was a no-brainer. This is
the chart he drew:

STAYING IN	CASHING OUT
Work	No Work
Schedule	No Schedule
Group Financial Accountability	Personal Financial Freedom
Little Free Time	All Free Time

The bottom line—the logical addition of all the separate pieces of information—was this: Rogers was one of the fortunate few. He was about to
embark on the Great American Dream.

Yet for some reason, Rogers experienced flutters of intuition, nagging
whispers in his soul. *Better be safe. Hedge your bets. Nail some confirmation.* So
he set up a dinner with three of his friends, all of whom had sold their busi-

nesses and retired within the previous five years. Like him, they were followers of Christ, interested in devoting their time and resources to something "more spiritual"—family, church, soul development. Rogers expected a good rack of lamb, toasts with a full-bodied Bordeaux, and words of astonishing encouragement: "Go, Rogers, this is it! The life you have been looking for—pleasure, satisfaction, fulfillment!" The dinner's greatest danger: In between great laughs, he might unexpectedly choke on a piece of warm bread.

During the appetizers one of the friends asked, "So what's the news, Rogers? Didn't you say this was a celebration dinner?"

"Thought you'd never ask," Rogers said, breaking into a timid smile.

"Let me guess: you just won a $100 million lottery?" his friend said.

"Not quite. But the next best thing." Rogers paused a moment to build a little suspense before continuing. "Got an offer to buy my company. Looks like a great deal."

A chorus of congratulations came from all around. Then the three friends reeled off the typical questions: "Who's the buyer?" "How did they find you?" "What's the courtship been like?" "Are they going to keep your management team?" "How do your people feel about that?" "Are you going to get your asking price?"

He answered them all and then took his time on the last one. That was the best part of all. "And yes, we're talking pretty close to my original asking price."

Once again, they all nodded approval. The Great American Dream—Rogers savored the moment. He'd finally been nominated to join their club.

"So, are you really going to cash out?" one of them pressed.

"Well, I'm very seriously considering it." *Of course I am!* he thought. *Why wouldn't I?*

"Have you lined up what you'll do next?" his friend asked.

"Not exactly. But the way I see it, I'll be real comfortable while I'm trying to figure that out." He raised his glass. "That's why I'm buying dinner—so you guys can tell me what's next."

"Don't look at me," his friend said.

Rogers glanced at the other two. They in turn shrugged, took another sip, and averted their eyes.

Rogers repeated, "So tell me what I can look forward to after I cash their check."

Again, uncomfortable stares, stammers, mumbles. In the next half-hour,

Rogers listened. Carefully. More carefully than he'd listened to anybody in a long time. Two of the three men had new wives. All three had spent tons of money on new toys—a bigger car, a bigger boat, a bigger plane. Rogers clearly heard their messages: *I am in a crisis of soul—a crisis of meaning.*

Rogers Kirven quickly lost his appetite: he—Rogers Kirven, almost in the top 1 percent of the nation's wealthiest.

Of Curses and Four-Letter Words

Work, perhaps, has become the ultimate obscenity, the filthiest of the four-letter words. Think of the menacing, mocking smile implicit in some of its synonyms: labor, chore, duty, job, and toil. *Labor*, as in childbirth. *Chore*, innately and inanely unpleasant. *Duty*, as in "You simply must." *Job*, a polite but still unavoidably crude, word for potty training. *Toil*—sounds like the old witch incantation, "Bubble, bubble, toil and trouble." Try this: Say the word *work* on a weekend, maybe in the middle of a Broncos/Niners game or while shopping the countryside for antiques, and see if you don't get the same look as if you had just thrown a four-day-dead raccoon onto the living room floor. Those four little letters have become the antithesis of blasphemy, of Life As It Should Be.

If you doubt the accuracy of the negative overtones of work, check out Mr. Roget's antonyms for work: *leisure, rest, repose, recreation.* You could easily fall into a peaceful sleep on a rainy mid-May afternoon meditating on such fundamentally relaxing opposites.

Work, then, isn't fun, but it feeds the bulldog. Not to mention the family. Real Life, however, happens elsewhere, outside of a cubicle or a windowless office or even a top-floor penthouse suite overlooking the carefully manicured, perfectly blossom-lined symmetry of corporate headquarters. That's what most of us believe. The best we can do is set goals, burn the adrenaline, and on some future day—hopefully sooner than later—arrive at the shore of our dreams, hopefully with a 42 Bertram Twin 375 in tow, rigged to the nines.

Crises of Meaning

My wife and I (Tom) glimpsed this coming reality back during graduate school, when we earned extra bucks housesitting for the families in the affluent Lake Forest area of our city. These families would jet off with their golf clubs to Hawaii for a few rounds. Then they'd fly to Greece for a day-and-a-half meeting. Then on to Paris for a month's vacation. But as we drove them to the airport and picked them up on their return, we seemed always to catch them in an argument with each other. They were unhappy when they left; they were unhappy when they returned. And it didn't take us long to understand that these families probably were unhappy in the middle. The writer of Ecclesiastes did not deny that people can find pleasure; what he did deny is that pleasure and a paycheck bring fulfillment. Both also can deepen the feeling of fragmentation and crises of the soul.

But don't take our observations alone for the truth. Ask Rogers Kirven. He did not cash out. His dinner guests' reports shook him that badly. Instead, he took a 100 percent stock option, no money, and continued working. Rogers, though, was not completely willing to let the Great American Dream slip away, at least not without another hearing. He is a man who always seeks out second—if not third and fourth—opinions. He is a self-admitted research junkie. He had to rule out the possibility that his three miserable cashed-out, soul-crushed friends were the exception, not the rule.

Since his buyout offer three years ago, Rogers has conducted interviews with thirty-six different people who decided to sell their businesses. The men—all between the ages of thirty and fifty, and with a liquid cash value between $5 and $35 million dollars—were nearly all, in Kirven's words, "universally depressed."

Of the thirty-six interviewed, thirty-three had divorced since their buyouts. The average age of the second wives: twenty-three. Nearly all had flashed through the following "I'm bored with this toy" cycle—golf: six months; new car: six to nine months; great big boat: one-and-a-half years. Most of them, in fact, were spending *less* time with family and on personal development—some of the very reasons why most of them had decided to cash out in the first place. Although each of them said they had a strategy for Life After Cash Out, it quickly disappeared in the rushing torrent of change. In the words of Mike Tyson: "They all have a strategy until they get hit." Of the thirty-six interviewed, twelve were self-proclaimed followers of Christ. Yet virtually no difference existed in the catastrophic nature of their statistics.

They all had experienced a deep "crisis of meaning." One piece of their lives seemed desperately absent.

Fragments of Ruin

In a postmodern world, hung over on efficiency, we whisper the word quietly, half in desperation, half in hope: *whole*.

We are tired of lives committed to the perfectly fragmented: a man who makes $2.5 million a year and spends no time with his family. An ultralight backpacker with titanium ice screws, continuous baffles, and microfleece, yet not one single ounce of work ethic. A religious fundamentalist, strung out on dogma, who can't seem to muster an ounce of love. A mother who can name the local members of the PTO and the NEA and the NTA, but has rarely been a student of a sunset. We are surprised (but not too surprised) when we read that the list of support groups includes sessions for those "addicted" to chocolate, cluttering, stealing, adrenaline, sex, junk food, gambling, religion, and support groups. We are sick of trumpeting one-dimensional success stories that permit and hide layers and layers of profound failure.

> Wholeness, we have come to believe, is impossible because it involves the integration of such imperfect parts. So as a compromise, we go off on a quest for the Perfect Fragment.

And we are tired—bone tired—of the incessant, gnawing feeling of never measuring up. Experts haunt and intimidate us. Some experts say we would need more than 80 hours in a day to accomplish the minimum activity requirements suggested by experts—things we *should* be doing to be a true success. In every area of life—family, social, education, work, religion, fitness, finances, recreation—the individual standards have been raised so high that "success" is virtually unachievable.

If you wish to make money, then measure yourself against Bill Gates. If you want to be physically fit, take a look at the pecs of Jean Claude Van Damme. If you want to be a spiritual giant, consider the tiny Mother Teresa. And if you want to be a homemaker, gawk at the kitchen of Martha Stewart. Success—the kind our culture promotes and glorifies—is mostly defined by a unilateral obsession that, in the end, costs nothing less than our humanity.

The Perfect Fragment

Most of us live—whether we admit it or not—terribly unbalanced lives. Wholeness, we have come to believe, is impossible because it involves the integration of such imperfect parts. So as a compromise, we go off on a quest for the Perfect Fragment. If we just had the time to stand back and examine our lives, we would see that it is a terribly bizarre way to live.

Imagine a woman who sets out to build the Perfect House. She decides, say, to begin design on the kitchen. She does her kitchen research: subscribing to all the magazines, tuning in to *Kitchens of the Rich and Famous*, searching the Internet for "quintessential kitchens," and hiring the best architects. She puts in long hours and spends many, many dollars. Finally, it is time to build. The chosen architect arrives, and the following conversation takes place:

"Here is what it will take to build the Perfect Kitchen," the architect says, whispering an outrageous figure in the woman's ear.

At first, she is speechless. Finally, she stammers out a few words: "But that would take all of the money I could make during the rest of my life."

The architect smiles. "I know."

"Well, this is just a kitchen. I still have to build the rest of the house."

"I know."

In desperation, she cries out, "Then what are my options?"

"Well," the architect begins, "the way I see it, you have two choices: you can build the Perfect Kitchen or a Mediocre House. That's about it."

A pause. She ponders, rolling the adjectives around in her head: *best* or *mediocre*. In the end, she decides, there is no real decision. *Best*—limited and myopic as it might be—always beats the socks off of *mediocre*.

And the soul shrinks.

In his epic poem, *The Wasteland*, T. S. Eliot put it a little more artistically: "I have shored these fragments against my ruin."[1] To survive in today's culture, you choose to divide your life into compartments—work, family, religion, community—and for the sake of sanity, try not to spend too much time figuring out what one has to do with another. Time, we are told, is one's most precious and rare commodity. You must, above all, stay narrowly focused.

We are exaggerating, of course. Few of us have become that soul-callused; but the pressures, nearly everyone would admit, are forcefully present. Moral schizophrenia becomes a clearly attractive option; integrity can now painlessly be dissected from real life. Achievement in some organizations demands as much.

Rogers Kirven has observed achievement from both sides, before and after. He knows the adrenaline-soaked, single-minded, all-consuming drive toward the Grand Goal. He has heard, too, of the other side: the maddening realization of illusion, the Grand Failure of the Grand Goal, and the unwanted, magnifying, and debilitating symptom of flawed character and soul. He does not understand why the disillusionment occurs, but he is desperate to find out. At the very least, it is a complex issue. He suspects it has something to do with "below the water line" issues: character as essential, not simply pragmatic, and work as intrinsically and powerfully valuable, not profoundly analgesic.

For Kirven, his research on "cash-out catastrophes" has served as a wake-up call. He has had to ask himself some soul-rending questions, such as: *Is life graded subject by subject, or by a composite score?*

In our current fragmented way of life, people can't do it all, so they "pick one" in the hierarchy of priorities. Some people select family. They're never dependable at the church and they're unfocused at work, but they're Superdads or Supermoms. Some people select church. They sell insurance on the side, just enough to cover the bills, but they basically work at the church. Some people select work. They spasmodically participate in the big events at church and show up for the really important family events, but they make success at work their consuming passion.

> In our current fragmented way of life, people can't do it all, so they "pick one" in the hierarchy of priorities.

But to be biblical about these priorities and hierarchies, you'll discover that you have to juggle all of these and give yourself one report card. It's much like going off to college and earning an A in French and flunking math, English, biology, and history. You won't stay in school long, or get a broad education. Occasionally, the church even leads us astray, making us think that our grade in church or family is all that counts. But if we examine the truth articulated in Ecclesiastes, we discover that there are seasons and times for everything: a time to reap and a time to sow; a time to laugh and a time to cry; a time to give more priority to work and less to family; a time to give more priority to family and less to work.

Consider Nehemiah's assignment. He was tasked with building a wall. It took him fifty-two days, working around the clock. Burning the candle at both ends, he and his workers were unapologetically consumed with their task. No eight-hour days then. It was 24/7/52. Likewise, in our lives we often experience seasonal assignments: building a new business, finishing a college degree, or raising funds for a community project that consumes six months or two years of our lives.

But examine the rest of the book. That's not the way Nehemiah and his crew lived life routinely. The work priority was only for a season. The peculiar danger to followers of Jesus here is that when God has called them to a task that they love, they forget the other balls that God has asked them to juggle.

Tom Muccio, a senior vice president with Procter and Gamble in charge of customer business development worldwide, under-stands the composite-score concept. And when he interviews and hires staff, he makes it his responsi-bility to get to know the entire person, not just his or her work persona. His recognition-and-reward system works the same way. Sitting on his desk are his ten "personal operating philosophies/expec-tations" that evidence his attention to the whole person he expects his direct reports to be. According to his employees, he's the master of creating and maintaining a corporate culture that makes people feel as though they're cared for and expected to live integrated lives. In fact, Tom refers to this wholeness concept as the "secret side of the secret weapon of business success."

> Life is about putting Humpty Dumpty together again.

In this, our postmodern world, life is about putting Humpty Dumpty together again. About becoming a whole person inside. About inviting God into all facets of a full life and moving seamlessly from one subject or season to the next.

Falling to Pieces

Not everyone buys into the concept. A few would paint a different picture. Some researchers would argue that the twentieth century represents the greatest era of progress known to humanity around the world, that we've achieved more in the last hundred years than in all the previous centuries combined.

Life expectancy has increased by thirty years, from forty-seven to seventy-seven. Infant mortality rates have fallen tenfold, from one hundred to seven per one thousand live births. The number of deaths from major diseases (tuberculosis, polio, typhus, whooping cough, and pneumonia) has fallen to fewer than fifty per one hundred thousand. Air quality has improved by about 30 percent in major cities since 1977. Agricultural productivity has risen five- to tenfold. Real per capita gross domestic product has risen from $4,800 to $31,500. And real manufacturing wages have moved from $3.45 an hour to $12.50 an hour. The poverty rate has decreased from 40 percent to 13 percent of U.S. households. The patents granted have increased from 25,000 to 150,000. Education has risen from 22 percent to 88 percent of adults completing high school. Computer ownership has increased from 1 percent of U.S. households in 1980 to 44 percent today.[2]

But are economic advances—and even health benefits—the only, or even the primary, yardstick? Other social trends indicate big rips in the fabric of our society's psyche: increases in family breakups, in abortions, in illegitimate births, in teen suicides, in violent crimes in our schools and in our workplaces. As we grow more prosperous from our work, we are growing more alienated from our friends, our families, and our God.

This fragmentation of life, most sociologists and theologians agree, can be traced to the Industrial Revolution. In 1776, as we pointed out in the previous chapter, Adam Smith published his book *The Wealth of Nations: An Inquiry into the Nature and Causes,* which set the philosophical groundwork for a dramatic change in the nature of work and, in turn, how human life was experienced.

Smith, the world's first industrial engineer, argued that work should be "segmented." Up to that point in history, workers were generally involved in the "wholeness" of task; in other words, a carpenter cut the tree, lathed and planed the wood, built the wheel, and installed it on the oxen-yoked, broken-down wagon. He was with the job from beginning to end. He saw the wholeness of a task.

Smith argued that the process of work involved a great deal of inherent waste. Time and energy were lost as the carpenter walked the woods looking for the right tree, changed from planer to hammer to clamp, and traveled again from shop to field. The time and energy lost in each chore by each worker, multiplied over time, was, he reasoned, enormous and terribly inefficient. The solution would be to fragment the work into individual tasks performed by individual workers. In essence, Smith pitted efficiency against wholeness.

The world would never be the same.

In many ways, Smith's idea of the division of labor was brilliant. It allowed people gifted to do a particular task to perform skillfully and in a timely manner. People enjoyed depth at the expense of breadth. Yet even Smith warned of potential dangers. Individuals, he warned, could be stripped of their essential value as people and reduced to mere units of production. Unfortunately, Smith's prophetic warnings were largely neglected.

Work, as he predicted, often became "just a job," a way to earn a living, but divorced from what real life was supposed to be. Work became a fragment of existence, a separate, disconnected, and often unpleasant way to spend a Wednesday.

Ironically, the rugged individualism so critical in building the United States into a world superpower also played a key role in fragmenting our lives. America, stripped of the need for any other individual or any other country, went from New World Infant to Nouveau-Rich World Power on the strength of its can-do individualism.

The downside, however, was that culture developed into one big group of people who were losing interest in working, or living, together. Instead of bonding tightly with an external family, for instance, the typical American teenager was just as likely to set off on her own, moving cross-country for college or career. This wasn't all bad; in fact, in many ways it was very good. But there was a price.

Church, too, became a retreat, something people withdrew into, to connect with other believers before going back out into the pagan world. We need connection and association with other believers, of course, but often churches create a sense of fragmentation in their members, making them feel guilty for or depressed about having to go "back out into the world." Some ministries have their entire focus on only one role of our lives: wife, husband, single, parent, student. Inherent in such a single focus, however, is the one-dimensional pull, the fragmented feel.

Other churches, like Bill Hybels's Willow Creek Community Church in Chicago, work for integration, a sense of wholeness for the individual. Willow Creek might be considered a church department store; every role people play in life can be bolstered through its ministry. Bill Hybels has found a way to make the workplace the distribution center for the gospel because that's where the energy already flows. But churches ministering to the whole person are still the exception, not the rule.

A few leading-edge companies also are working for integration. DuPont CEO and President John A. Krol says of his company's observations and family programs for child and elder care, "Work-life programs are a power-ful tool to motivate people and encourage commitment to achieving business objec-tives."[3] Wal-Mart contracts with Resources for Living to assist its employees with life crises or questions. Trilogy Software in Texas owns ski boats on Austin's Horseshoe Bay that are available to employ-ees at any time for stress release. J. C. Penney provides on-site day-care facil-ities so that parents can have lunch with their children in the company cafeteria and check on them throughout the day. Such programs represent a fundamental shift toward making work an integral part of all of life, not a separate segment. But again, these are the exceptions, not the rule.

> Life is a matter of connecting to God, others, beauty, and love in all our settings, work or otherwise.

In the 1996 bestseller *Habits of the Heart: Individualism and Commitment in America*, a team of sociologists put it this way:

> The most distinctive aspect of 20th century American society is the division of life into a number of separate functional sectors: home and workplace, work and leisure, white collar and blue collar, public and pri-vate. This division suited the needs of the bureaucratic industrial cor-porations that provided the model for our preferred means of organizing society by the balancing and linking of sectors as "depart-ments."[4]

In fact, it's not unusual to hear people make the analogy in casual con-versation: "I'm not doing too well in the parenting department; my teen is driving me nuts." Or: "Over in the financial department, my spouse and I are behind. We don't have diddly-squat in savings." We've transferred this business lingo of fragmentation to describe every aspect of our lives.

Particularly powerful in molding our contemporary sense of things has been the division between various "tracks" to achievement laid out in schools, corporations, government, and the professions, on the one hand, and the balancing life-sectors of home, personal ties, and "leisure" on the other.

The fragmentation of life—the ever-increasing breakdown of life and living into "workable" categories—has become the standard *modus operandi*. Life, once valued for its wholeness and integration, is literally falling to pieces: categories, fragments, and disconnected realities.

Abundant Life and the Call of God

Jesus spoke of abundance and wholeness. "I have come," he said, "that they may have life, and have it to the full" (John 10:10). At another time, he spoke with great exuberance: "Give, and it will be given to you. A good measure, pressed down, shaken together and running over, will be poured into your lap" (Luke 6:38). In his words you get a sense of wholeness, overflow, and gift, which stand in stark contrast to the current obsessions with focus, control, and one-dimensional achievement. His words promise surprising integration. Life—in all of its multifaceted, brilliant hues and sublime layers—is whole. Life is a matter of connecting to God, others, beauty, and love in *all* our settings, work or otherwise.

In *The Call*, Os Guinness writes:

> Calling is the truth that God calls us to Himself so decisively that everything we are, everything we do, and everything we have is invested with a special devotion and dynamism lived out as a response to His summons and service. . . . Little wonder that the rediscovery of calling should be critical today, not least in satisfying the passion for purpose of millions of questioning modern people.[5]

The call of God, then, is not to a fragmented life of at best, one-dimensional success, but to a balanced and whole existence fully and dynamically alive in God's grace and love. In "everything we are, everything we do, and everything we have," we are called to God. True success is multidimensional, experienced fully across *all* of the dimensions of human existence: government, church, work, home.

What would that wholeness look like?

It looks like Ken Edmundson. Ken, an elder in his church and well-respected in his community, at forty-seven has a composite score that ranks near the top. He's built and sold several very large businesses over the past twenty years, including an aviation services business sold to a major airline and a national apartment company with 55,000 apartments around the country sold to a Wall Street firm. And all the while, he has managed to build a solid marriage and parent three great girls. Through the years, he has managed to find time to go to dad-and-daughter camps and make Wednesdays Date Night with a different daughter each week. Here's a guy who's doing things right, pulling together all the pieces into a whole, abundant life. He's the benefactor of a life well spent, with God clearly infused into all arenas: at work, at home, at church, in the community.

The composite score goes down in the record book.

Naming the New World

Columbus and Vespucci died disappointed men. Despite the fact that they had unknowingly discovered a vast new continent with unimaginable riches and resources, they considered their missions a failure: they never found the passage to the "Indies," a source of proven treasure. In a sense, they failed to recognize the land they kept running into as a new and stunning frontier and not merely an obstacle.

In today's world, the new—or at least rediscovered frontier—is the institution of work. And it should not be an obstacle to an abundant life. People want their work to amount for more than a weekly paycheck. They want their work to matter. They want their work to integrate seamlessly into their rhythm of life. The current business environment, going through an unequalled phase of transition, no longer stands as a barrier. Words like *spirituality, fulfillment,* and *community* are now heard across board rooms and in teleconferences as often as the old standards of *profit, bottom line,* and *production.*

> The fragmented life appears simple, filled with focus on a few select pursuits. But in reality it is complex, filled with stress and disappointment. The whole life appears complicated, filled with spinning plates and a juggler's bowling pins. But in reality it is simple, filled with natural rhythms that generate fulfillment.

For example, take a look at Tom Muccio's "personal operating philosophies/expectations" for his new hires; under "planning" he refers employees once again to spiritual truths:

- "Any enterprise is built by wise planning, becomes strong through common sense, and profits wonderfully by keeping abreast of the facts" (Prov. 24:3–4 TLB).
- You reap what you sow.
- Trees and people are identified by the fruit they produce.

To get to the promised land in the Fourth Frontier, we must set out to discover something more—to explore what's *really there.*

In the time of Columbus and Vespucci, the Old World simply was not prepared for any sort of New World. Europeans were not ready to accept, as yet, that a startling frontier—a fourth part of the world—was a reality. In *The Discoverers*, Daniel Boorstin wrote of their stubborn refusal to claim the new land for what it was:

> It is not surprising that the newness of the New World, with all its unimagined opportunities, did not take Europe by storm. Booksellers and mapmakers had a vested interest in the supposed accuracy of items on their shelves and in the wood blocks and plates from which these were made. The most respectable maps, and globes, and planispheres had left no room at all for a Fourth Continent. The vocabulary of the papal bulls and the administrative forms of government departments all encouraged people to stay in linguistic ruts. Since Columbus had "discovered" those lands in the "Indies," it seemed prudent as well as convenient to keep thinking of the new overseas empire in that way and not to give it the legally perilous implications which a newfangled name might suggest.[6]

The fourth continent eventually was named after Amerigo Vespucci, even though he didn't believe he'd actually discovered a new world and despite the fact he'd arrived on its shore almost a decade after Christopher Columbus. This is encouraging. It proves that grace exists for explorers.

Life Today: Simple or Complex?

Sarah Ban Breathnach took the publishing world by storm with her best-seller *Simple Abundance.* Could she be correct, readers wondered, with her paradoxical title? The fragmented life is a paradoxical reality of the modern human condition. The fragmented life appears simple, filled with focus on a few select pursuits. But in reality it is complex, filled with stress and disappointment. The whole life appears complicated, filled with spinning plates and a juggler's bowling pins. But in reality it is simple, filled with natural rhythms that generate fulfillment.

People seem to sense this reality, as if something from deep within calls them. They desire wholeness precisely because people were created in the image of God, who is whole in every sense of the word. People crave wholeness just as they crave an understanding of and a relationship with the living God. And yet the fragmented life grows like kudzu.

The good news: we learned to be fragmented, and we can unlearn it. Societies have a history of buying into some rather obvious lies, of looking at the temporal and ignoring the eternal to the point of their own damnation. Only in hindsight, and sometimes not even then, do we spot the folly of our misplaced ambitions. The excuse, when looking back at a long and fragmented life, isn't that there was no desire to change, but rather that there was no game plan for change.

> The excuse, when looking back at a long and fragmented life, isn't that there was no desire to change, but rather that there was no game plan for change.

Jesus is the solution—a whole-life solution to the problem of fragmentation. He is the spiritual reality of wholeness, the antidote to the fragmented life. "Come to me, all you who are weary and burdened, and I will give you rest. Take my yoke upon you and learn from me, for I am gentle and humble in heart, and you will find rest for your souls. For my yoke is easy and my burden is light" (Matt. 11:28–30).

We promised to tell it like it is—to write about today's marketplace as it really exists. Reality. What, then, are the six realities of the Fourth Frontier that, properly understood, are key to having life "to the full"? Consider marriage for a moment. Do your research on the qualities of a happy, Christ-centered marriage, and you'll find the same ingredients common to all: purity. Intimacy. Communication. Selfless love.

Likewise, certain realities rise to the top of any discussion of Christ-centered work: devotion. Calling. Integrity. Stewardship. Rest. Colonization. In the next six chapters, we'll take a look at each of these realities represented in a whole, integrated life. Spend some time with men and women who live and breathe a "very, very" life (the final chapter), and observe these six realities as an unmistakably visible part of their abundant life.

Forget the vitamin pill to pull you through the fragmented life; let's go for the meat and vegetables that produce a healthy mindset and a God-connection to your whole existence. Watch work melt from fragment to part of the whole.

PART III

SIX REALITIES OF
THE FOURTH FRONTIER

5

THE TRIP FROM WITHIN:
DETERMINING YOUR DEVOTION

THE ANGRY WATERS of the Mediterranean Sea pounded the ancient vessel, crashing wave upon wave against a wooden hull that soon, it seemed, would splinter and sink, or perhaps, float the raging whitecaps to the beaches of some distant shore. The crew was experienced, and its duty was to calm the fears of passengers who were accustomed to calmer waters. But Monica needed no such assurance. Indeed, it was Monica, filled with a deep, inner peace that came with her faith, who calmly promised the sailors that everything would be just fine.

Her son, meanwhile, faced his own stormy seas. At his home in Italy awaiting his mother's arrival from Africa, Aurelius Augustinus was in "a dangerous state of depression." The cause: "I had lost all hope of discovering truth." [1] He still desperately was searching for what his mother long ago had found—truth.

Nothing excited or depressed Augustine quite like the exploration of his inner being, his quest for truth. In this regard, he was perhaps the greatest explorer of all time, a man on a mission who for years found himself dissatisfied with wherever he was but convinced the next town on his trip would be Utopia. While his mother had pursued a devout faith in Jesus for most of her life, Augustine spent many of his adult years trying to find his own path home.

And it was some path. Augustine was born in 354 in what was the Roman province of Numidia (it is now eastern Algeria). His father was a Roman pagan; his mother, a devout Christian. Augustine's sharp mind and thirst for knowledge led to a career as a teacher. An avid reader and a lifelong student, he pored over the various philosophical teachings of his day in a vain attempt to understand good and evil, sin and virtue, heaven and hell. In his youth, he "ran wild in the shadowy jungle of erotic adventures," and for fifteen years he kept a concubine.[2] But intellectually he continually struggled to understand his carnal lust.

Augustine had been raised in the church, but he found the Old Latin version of the Bible uninviting. As a young adult, he was drawn more to the works of Mani, a third-century Gnostic. Followers of Mani, known as Manichees, strongly denied the historical crucifixion of Jesus, relied heavily on astronomy for guidance, and held the physical world, and especially the act of human reproduction, in contempt. While few embraced abstinence, the Manichees felt strongly that procreation was the ultimate misuse of sexual activity. The more Augustine explored this faith, however, the less it satisfied his soul. He was living in Milan with his concubine and his illegitimate son when his mother found him in a state of depression over his spiritual journey. Roughly a decade after he had embraced it, Augustine had given up the Manichee mythology and was set to renew his search for truth. As he wrote in Confessions:

> I myself was exceedingly astonished as I anxiously reflected how long a time had elapsed since the nineteenth year of my life, when I began to burn with a zeal for wisdom. . . . And here I was already thirty, and still mucking about in the same mire in a state of indecision . . . saying: "Tomorrow I shall find it; see it, it will become perfectly clear, and I shall have no more doubts."[3]

Mathematics became his next religion. There were no certainties, he reasoned, beyond pure mathematics. Then he began to read the works of Plotinus, a Roman philosopher who taught a century before him. But Augustine's attempts to achieve a union with God through a transience experience were disappointing.

While still in Milan, however, his mother introduced him to the teachings of Ambrose, a Christian bishop whom he grew to respect for both his spiritual and intellectual natures. Augustine still was experimenting with other philosophies, but seeds of influence were planted. In the summer of 386, Augustine was in a garden waging an internal debate regarding his spiritual journey. He felt so trapped by the sins of his past that he broke down in tears. Alone, he heard the voice of a child chanting, "Pick up and read, pick up and read." He interpreted it as a divine command, so he found his Bible, opened it, and began to read: "Let us behave decently, as in the daytime, not in orgies and drunkenness, not in sexual immorality and debauchery, not in dissension and jealousy. Rather, clothe yourselves with the Lord Jesus Christ, and do not think about how to gratify the desires of the sinful nature" (Rom. 13:13–14).

"I neither wished nor needed to read further," Augustine would write of his conversion. "At once, with the last words of this sentence, it was as if a light of relief from all anxiety flooded into my heart. All the shadows of doubt were dispelled."[4]

The following Easter, Augustine was baptized. His mother, Monica, a lifelong follower of Christ, lived to see her son's conversion. She died a few years later, her prayers answered, Augustine's journey "home" complete.

Augustine's search had ended, but his exploration—his devotion to his faith—had just begun. Augustine embraced Christ with a passion, eventually was ordained, and later became bishop of Hippo. His writings, in particular Confessions and City of God, have become classics of the faith and of Western literature.

The Chasm Between What We Say and What We Do

We're a nation of people who say one thing and do another. A 1999 study released by Barna Research Group, an independent marketing research company in Ventura, California, shows that during the past nine years there has been relatively little change in our Christian values and beliefs. What has changed is the *practice* of those beliefs. The data demonstrate that the bulk of Christian commitment has been in the way we live out those beliefs Monday to Monday. Worship attendance, Bible reading, and prayer showed the largest drops in Christian practices.[5]

George Barna, president of the research firm that released the study, points out the paradoxes in this survey of one thousand adults in forty-eight states:

> Sometimes it's easy to lose sight of the true spiritual character of our nation. More than four out of five adults call themselves "Christian," but these figures raise questions about what that term means for many people. . . . Those who suggest that Americans are becoming more conservative, more traditional, and more religious should recognize that these data describe a nation that is not becoming more Biblically informed, more spiritually mature, or more authentically Christian.[6]

But what about the younger generation? Don't the media, in the wake of such recent violence in schools across the country, report that groups of Christian teens are praying to God for answers to this rash of violence in their midst?

A January 2000 study, also conducted by Barna Research Group, indicates that the relationship most teens have with Christianity seems superficial. According to their responses on the survey, neither their beliefs nor their practices demonstrate a deep commitment to Christ. Although their religious actions seem more overt than those of the Baby Boomers, their commitment seems even less so. Less than two-thirds (64 percent) describe themselves as "religious." Only three out of five call themselves "spiritual," and only the same proportion (60 percent) say they are committed Christians. Of these 60 percent who say classify themselves as "committed Christians," only half qualify as born-again Christians, having "made a personal commitment to Jesus Christ that is still important in their lives today."[7]

"Being deeply committed to the Christian faith" ranked in the bottom third of nineteen "desirable outcomes" for their future. "Being personally active in a church" ranked even lower, at sixteenth. Strong relationships and lifestyle comforts ranked much higher than religious outcomes for their life.[8]

> We as Americans think we're religious. We even label ourselves "committed, born-again Christians." Yet we don't agree on what that commitment looks like in daily life.

Although two out of three feel a strong desire to have a personal relationship with God, only four out of ten of these "believers in Jesus" are active in their church. Only one in four (26 percent) says he or she is "absolutely committed to the Christian faith."[9]

In this new report (based on interviews with 2,867 teens over the last three years) by George Barna, which is entitled *Third Millennium Teens,* these youth are a study in contradictions. While they want to be considered "religious," they plan to invest little of themselves in that spiritual pursuit. Currently, only 4 percent of American teens fit the evangelical criteria.[10]

But aging changes the picture. According to a special analysis of Gallup Poll data collected nationally from 1992 to 1999, including interviews with more than forty thousand national adults, religious interest and involvement increases in later years of life. Church attendance and other indicators of faith increase with age.[11]

What do we make of all this data? We as Americans think we're religious. We even label ourselves "committed, born-again Christians." Yet we don't agree on what that commitment looks like in daily life.

The bigger issue: When we face dilemmas, crises, and daily lifestyle choices, we have a weak foundation upon which to build an abundant, meaningful life. So where to start? In a word, *devotion*.

A Portrait of Devotion

Gordon Addington, my (Tom's) dad, was ten years old when his parents first presented him with a Bible of his very own. It was in the thirties, and many churches in America at that time were pushing followers to read through the Bible in a year. So as a new year dawned, young Gordon began to read. He bogged down in Leviticus and Numbers, and some of it—perhaps much of it—didn't make much sense, but eventually he conquered the Old Testament and plowed right on through to the end of Revelation.

More than sixty years later, after a successful career as a surgeon that took him from St. Paul, Minnesota, to Hong Kong and back, Gordon considers that year the start of an intentional devotion to Christ, a process of attempting to learn what God had to say and of following through on what he understood. That early and continuing devotion has determined his actions for life. Everything he did, from the way he treated his wife and raised his family, to the Bible studies he led, to the way he treated patients and colleagues, to his work around the world as a missionary, was rooted in his daily devotion to God.

The same is true of Augustine's mother, Monica. After she arrived in Italy, Monica took cakes, bread, and wine to the memorial shrines, as had been her custom at home in Africa. But officials quickly informed her that the practice was not allowed in Milan. "When she knew that the bishop was responsible for the prohibition," Augustine would later write of his mother, "she accepted it in so devout and docile a manner that I myself was amazed how easy it was for her to find fault with her own custom rather than to dispute his ban. . . . Her quest was for devotion, not pleasure."[12]

> Devotion, as Augustine discovered, has little value if not focused on Christ.

Devotion describes a deepening inner experience with Jesus—rooted in expanding knowledge of him, increasing communication with him, and growing love for him. Devotion results in progressive life change, exploring and living out what we discover in communion with Christ.

After Augustine's conversion, his mother's inner devotion and outward practice spoke volumes to him. Whenever Augustine wrote of his mother, he consistently commented on her devotion to God, of her desire to know God more closely so that she could mature spiritually with each new day. But devotion, as Augustine discovered, has little value if not focused on Christ.

The Focus of Our Devotion: Religion á la Carte

There is no shortage of spiritual language in today's marketplace. The problem is that much of this talk has no underpinnings of truth and light. Much of the talk is rooted in New Age philosophies or Eastern religions such as Hinduism. In this regard, the modern marketplace isn't much different from the fourth-century marketplace—street after street filled with merchants peddling faith á la carte.

Listen in on the conversations in boardrooms, hallways, and teleconferences of corporate America:

"I've got to take some time to center myself."

"Jeremy's going through a personal crisis, and I think as a team we should appeal to a higher power on his behalf."

"I intend to win that chunk of business; all it takes is imagining."

"I don't know, Rachel, about that promotion. Why don't you think it over a few days, connect with your inner spirit? See if it feels right. See if the idea excites or depresses you."

Sound familiar in your corner of the world?

Modern society insists that followers of Christ tolerate a variety of faiths, and, indeed, history tells us that forcing any belief system on people proves destructive and unfruitful. Yet society also suggests, and many followers of Christ accept, that we should embrace the relative truth of a multitude of faiths. Diversity in religion rests at the heart of postmodernism. The crux: There are many ways to God, each just as good as the other. Everything is relative. Nothing is absolute. And consequently, spirituality is a never-ending journey that travels innumerable paths.

Religion, with that mindset, is about the journey, not the foundation nor the destination.

But a life with Jesus is a one-of-a-kind solution, a one-and-only approach to a personal relationship with God. This life works equally well for anyone willing to embrace it—the rich, the poor; the young, the old; the tall, the short; the American, the Asian, the European. It is the end of the search, the beginning of the exploration. It begins when we come to the end of ourselves and embrace the undeserved yet unconditional grace of the Father.

Solomon, the wisest of the wise, learned this in much the same way that Augustine did centuries later. The son of King David tried all kinds of things to give meaning to his life: He expanded his earthly empire, earned the respect of foreign monarchs, oversaw majestic construction projects, grew the wealth of his kingdom, and passionately pursued—and found—physical pleasures. He was a brilliant leader, a man who had the world at his fingertips. He knew all about living for the moment. But as he points out in Ecclesiastes 3:11, God "has also set eternity in the hearts of men."

Something in the hearts of people everywhere yearns for a greater understanding of God. Solomon discovered that a life devoted to God brings fulfillment as nothing else can. This God-created void can be filled only by a relationship with Jesus. Much like Augustine hundreds of years later, Solomon discovered that peace resulted from devotion to God, not in wealth, achievement, or physical pleasures.

The pursuit of that understanding can take many different forms, but it has to be intentional and consistent. To integrate faith and work, we as followers of Christ must first devote our lives to Christ—wholeheartedly. There is no middle ground, no plethora of choices that expands or contracts with the tide of circumstances or rewards.

> The first step toward a deepening relationship with God is to do what he says—to obey his commands.

When the decision is between expedient or right, we choose right. When the decision is between serving people or deceiving them, we choose serving. When the decision is between investing in God's kingdom or our pleasure, we choose God's kingdom. When the decision is between speaking for God or remaining silent, we choose to speak.

Devotion dictates decisions. Always.

When Gordon Addington breaks down the meaning of devotion to Christ, he inevitably arrives at the word *love*. But if devotion is a love for God, what does it look like? Gordon finds his answer beginning in John 14:21, where Jesus said, "Whoever has my commands and obeys them, he is the one who loves me. He who loves me will be loved by my Father, and I too will love him and show myself to him."

The first step toward a deepening relationship with God is to do what he says—to obey his commands. And if we're willing to obey his explicit biblical commands, then God progressively shows himself to us. Two verses later, in John 14:23, Jesus said, "If anyone loves me, he will obey my teaching. My Father will love him, and we will come to him and make our home with him."

This devotion to walk in obedience to Christ also was evident in the life of Solomon's father, King David. While Solomon spent much of his time experimenting with pleasures, possessions, and power, David spent most of his life focusing on God. Consequently, God chose David to rule Israel not because of his physical abilities or his mental sharpness, but because of his heart (1 Sam. 16:7). Through all his trials and tribulations, through the incredible highs and depressing lows, David was a man after God's own heart (Acts 13:22). Never differentiating between his roles as shepherd, musician, soldier, king, or servant of the Most High, David displayed a consistent devotion for the heart of God.

When he sinned—and David committed some whoppers—his response was to seek forgiveness and to repair his broken relationship with God. Although his personal weaknesses led him to murder and commit adultery, he had a spiritual center. After he sinned and a godly prophet called him on it, we see a man whose heart for God drove him into utter despair of guilt and remorse. He longed for God to make his "home" within him once again. David praised God for his blessings, and he accepted God's sovereignty during hard times.

In David's Psalms, we see a guy who related to God in a passionate, emotional way. We see a man sitting on a rock talking to his best friend in intimate dialogues. It was his devotion to God that gave him a framework for understanding forgiveness and then moving forward. For him, devotion began as an inside thing—a heart tug. And that inward devotion to God poured out in his daily living.

In New Testament terms, David's devotion allowed him to walk with the Spirit. Devotion demands a continual renewal, a rebirth each day of an intense and insatiable longing to be in relationship—an intimate relationship—with God.

For Gordon Addington, devotion means reading the Bible, praying, worshiping, all in an intentional effort to know and do the will of God so that it permeates every decision of every waking hour. And yet many followers of Christ never practice these disciplines in even a nominal way. Consequently, they find themselves in the workplace—one of the most intense battle-grounds around—with no armor, no weapons.

A customer stops by the trade-show booth to chat about the presidential race, tossing out a few political opinions of his own. The undevoted believer has no knowledge of biblical teachings about the issues, and thus no sound Christian perspective to offer.

A boss insists on a policy that undermines the dignity of employees. The undevoted staffer has no idea why it doesn't "feel right" or how to express his disagreement with the policy.

Competitive pricing becomes the only obstacle in winning the project. The salesperson, an undevoted believer, walks into the trap of offering inferior quality without calling the substitution to the buyer's attention.

Devotion provides the armor for the workplace.

Few biblical characters participated in the battle of life with more armor, more weapons, than Paul. As Saul, he was not one of the good guys. But on the way to Damascus, something happened. He met Christ, and his world was never the same. Saul became Paul, and Paul became a picture of devotion to Christ. God reached down and grabbed him, and Paul spent the rest of his life

> Devotion isn't so much about *what* we do as it is about *why* we do it.

trying to grab God back. He awoke each day with a renewed sense of why he was living—to love Christ *again* in the new day. The objective of his life was Christ. The scope of his pursuit was unlimited.

Paul's devotion affected every single aspect of his life: his career, his travels, his sense of safety, his theology, his relationships. Devotion became his defense and his offense in every battle.

Solomon, David, and Paul, not to mention Aurelius Augustinus and Gordon Addington, were drawn to God in different ways, not because the government or the culture forced them to believe, but because of the void in their hearts. They searched in different ways and in different times. But they all arrived at the same distinct conclusion: God—the Father, the Son, and Holy Spirit—reigns supreme, and man's duty on earth is to glorify him.

Jesus, when summing up all the laws of the Old Testament, put it this way: "Love the Lord your God with all your heart and with all your soul and with all your mind" (Matt. 22:37). Everything else, again according to Ecclesiastes, is meaningless, a chasing after the wind.

The Practice of Our Devotion: These "Easy" Things

The alarm cracked the darkness precisely at 3:55 each morning, but Gordon Addington was the only one who heard it. That's because it didn't go off on his nightstand: it went off in his head. For about an hour each day, Gordon would read the Bible and spend time alone with God. Breakfast was served at 5:45, then he, his wife, and his ten children gathered to sing, read the Bible, and pray. By 6:30, with the sunshine breaking through the trees, he was off to the hospital, where time for intentional communion with God was measured in seconds, not minutes or hours.

The routine has been much the same for most of my dad's life, whether he was working his way through medical school, helping to start a missionary hospital in Hong Kong, or leading the surgery department at a hospital in Minnesota. As a child, I (Tom) can recall slipping out of bed in the middle of the night for a drink of water only to discover—sometimes in startling fashion—my father on his knees praying or reading his Bible. Even now well into his seventies, he starts most days by 5:30 in the peace and quiet of his study, immersed in a personal relationship with Christ.

> Paul's devotion to Christ started over each day. He lived present tense.

Rigid? Perhaps. He admits as much. But being a little rigid in the areas of spiritual discipline isn't necessarily a bad thing. Then again, Dad isn't trying to prove himself to the Lord. There have been times, in fact, when he didn't get up to pray, when he worked a thirty-six-hour shift that made it impossible for him to slip into his study for an hour of quiet time. As he puts it, "The Lord knows the schedule."

Devotion isn't so much about *what* we do as it is about *why* we do it. If devotion springs from a love for the Lord, then it doesn't become a dreaded chore or an all-controlling obsession. It's simply a part of life itself.

The essence of Paul's devotion to Christ wasn't all the things that he did for the cause of Christ. And it wasn't his conversion experience, an event so dramatic that it easily could have been the focus of everything he said and did for the rest of his life. No, Paul's devotion to Christ started over each day. He lived present tense.

Paul recognized, as evidenced in his letter to the Philippians, that devotion to Christ is an ongoing process, something that happens not once in a lifetime, but once every second: at church, at home, at work, in jail. Think for a moment about what Paul, while writing from a jail cell, told the Philippians about his personal devotion to Christ:

> Not that I have already . . . been made perfect, but I press on to take hold of that for which Christ Jesus took hold of me. Brothers, I do not consider myself yet to have taken hold of it. But one thing I do: Forgetting what is behind and straining toward what is ahead, I press on toward the goal to win the prize for which God has called me heavenward in Christ Jesus. (Phil. 3:12–14)

In his letters, Paul constantly invited other disciples of Christ to imitate him. But he didn't say, "Imitate the man I was two years ago." He said, "Imitate the man I am today." He took a present-tense approach to devotion.

Paul liked to compare a life with Christ to a race, one that required daily training in devotion.

> Everyone who competes in the games goes into strict training. They do it to get a crown that will not last; but we do it to get a crown that will last forever. Therefore I do not run like a man running aimlessly; I do not fight like a man beating the air. No, I beat my body and make it my slave so that after I have preached to others, I myself will not be disqualified for the prize. (1 Cor. 9:25–27)

Paul trained with purpose, with discipline, with devotion.

Many followers of Christ define devotion by pointing back to certain highlights: a week at summer camp as a teen, a great revival conversion, a personal retreat during a bewildering decision-point in life. Those are great memories and should not be taken for granted or dismissed. Those experiences provide meaningful stories for sharing God's transforming power with seekers.

But they have little to do with an individual, personal, daily devotion to Christ.

For Paul, devotion wasn't about only what happened yesterday, last week, or last year. To such stories, he might respond, "That's memorable. Now, what's happening in your life today? Why can't you get along with your brothers? How did you serve God last week in Cleveland? What are your plans for serving God next month at the convention?"

The plan? Passionate devotion.

The pattern? Repeated.

The time frame? Permanent.

For Dad, that training began as a preteen. It continued as he worked his way through high school, college, seminary, medical school, and his profes-

> Devotion is nothing less than an intense passion for Christ. That passion simply oozes out in actions every day.

sional career. But when Dad talks about devotion to Christ, he doesn't talk much about getting up early in the morning to read the Bible, memorizing Scripture, prayer, fasting, or meditation. Devotion is more than reading the Bible every morning at four o'clock or winning the attendance award at Bible Study Fellowship. Devotion is nothing less than an intense passion for Christ. That passion simply oozes out in these actions every day.

Devotion Determines Action

Devotion—this intense passion for the one-and-only solution to life—looks like action. It is the acknowledgement of Christ in every word, in every deed, in every action. Devotion seizes opportunities, eager to take command of a grand adventure.

The apostle Peter issued this call to action when he said, "Prepare your minds for action; be self-controlled; set your hope fully on the grace to be given you when Jesus Christ is revealed. As obedient children, do not conform to the evil desires you had when you lived in ignorance. But just as he who called you is holy, so be holy in all you do" (1 Peter 1:13–15).

Simply put, knowing the Bible backward and forward is meaningless if that knowledge doesn't result in action. On the other hand, we may have passionate emotion for God, but if we don't know the Bible, we won't fully experience God's plan for our lives.

Devotion involves merging the will of God—found through prayer, daily reading of the Bible, attention to the Holy Spirit—with action. In 2 Corinthians 5:14–21, Paul talked about relationships—our relationship with God and our relationship with other people. Near the end of those verses, he drew a connection: "We are therefore Christ's ambassadors, as though God were making his appeal through us. We implore you on Christ's behalf: Be reconciled to God" (2 Cor. 5:20). In other words, it is through an inner understanding of our relationship with God that we impact the world around us for Christ. So first we must cultivate that understanding, and then we must keep it on the tips of our tongues so that we can spring into action.

> Devotion doesn't start and end with a daily quiet time: It operates like a 7-11 store—full service, twenty-four hours a day.

Devotion doesn't start and end with a daily quiet time: It operates like a 7-11 store—full service, twenty-four hours a day.

A present-tense devotion showed up many times during Gordon Addington's professional career. There was the Christmas Day when he was making rounds at the hospital while we waited patiently for him to come home to celebrate around the tree.

"Dr. Addington?" a patient from his surgery ward called his name just as he turned to head out the door.

Dad stopped, waited.

The patient continued, "Lots of time on my hands these last few days. Makes me think about my life. Where I'm going. How I've lived. That kind of thing."

"The hospital's a good time for reflection," my dad told him, stepping back into the room. "You're right about that."

"What's the point, you know what I mean?" the patient continued.

Dad recognized the opportunity. Although attending to his temporal business, his heart was set on eternity. And while his family waited at home to celebrate Christmas with him, Dad spoke from his heart. The patient, broken no longer, made a decision to follow Christ, to embrace the One-and-Only's offer of undeserved salvation. And when Dad did get home to recount the bedside conversation, we understood devotion in action.

There was also the time a patient stopped Dad as he passed by her bed one morning on his way elsewhere.

"How come you do that every morning?" she asked.

Startled for a moment, Dad responded, "Do what, ma'am?"

"Whistling. Singing. Smiling. Humming. It's seven in the morning! How can you be so happy this early every day?"

Of course, he told her.

But there also was the occasion when Dad, pressed for time and in immediate need of a patient's x-ray, yelled to the technician, "Where's that x-ray for Baker?"

"I don't know, sir. I'll check on it." The x-ray technician hopped up from her paperwork and scurried off. She returned to report, "It's not ready yet."

"What do you mean, it's not ready? I sent her down ninety minutes ago!"

"We'll get to it as soon as possible, Dr. Addington."

"Well, that's not soon enough," Dad snapped. "I want it done, and I want it done *now*. Do you understand?" He turned on his heel and marched off.

Where was his devotion at this moment? Where was his intense intimate relationship with God? They reappeared a few hours later in the form of conviction. They grabbed him by the ear and dragged him to the x-ray department so he could apologize to the technician.

> Devotion to God provides the opposite of the old saying, "Garbage in, garbage out."

In a sense, devotion to God provides the opposite of the old saying, "Garbage in, garbage out." If we are filled with the love of God and an understanding of his will for mankind in general and for us as individuals, then people will see God in our every action—including our work.

Romans 8:5–10 ties it together:

> Those who live according to the sinful nature have their minds set on what that nature desires; but those who live in accordance with the Spirit have their minds set on what the Spirit desires. The mind of sinful man is death, but the mind controlled by the Spirit is life and peace; the sinful mind is hostile to God. It does not submit to God's law, nor can it do so. Those controlled by the sinful nature cannot please God.
>
> You, however, are controlled not by the sinful nature but by the Spirit, if the Spirit of God lives in you. And if anyone does not have the Spirit of Christ, he does not belong to Christ. But if Christ is in you, your body is dead because of sin, yet your spirit is alive because of righteousness.

Once we decide to devote our life to Christ, we no longer need to decide on our daily lifestyle. At that point, our duty is to manage the decision we've already made—to pursue God every day with the unbridled passion of a lover who has been granted eternity with the perfect partner: Christ Jesus.

Devotion Dictates the Details

Gordon Addington and Bob Chapman had arrived in Hong Kong with the idea of starting a clinic, but they soon discovered the need was for a hospital. Conditions were so severe, in fact, that newborn babies shared bassinets while their mothers shared hospital beds. Even in the infectious disease wards, the sick slept with the sick. As we mentioned in a previous chapter, the British government knew the need, and they offered free land for a hospital if my dad and Dr. Chapman could raise the funds and oversee the building.

Dad and Dr. Chapman had very little money and even fewer ideas. But when the Christian Medical Society introduced them to an influential visiting surgeon, C. Everett Koop, they began to see God's hand. Koop, in Japan to deliver a lecture, learned of their plans and of their need for funds. "Now I know why I came here," Koop told them, and he went to bat back in the States for them.

Soon the doctors received their requested $85,000 check. There was just one problem. By the time the check arrived, they realized it would not be enough. They had underestimated their needs by $35,000.

How could they ask for more? What other options did they have?

Administrators and bureaucrats turned the doctors down every step of the way: *request denied.* They appealed: *request denied.* They again appealed. Again, *request denied.* Finally, they made their third and last appeal. Dad and Mom sat by the phone, turning the matter over to God. The phone rang. My mom answered and listened intently as the caller said the third request had finally been approved.

"Praise the Lord!" Mom and Dad responded impulsively, with no thought of the man on the other end of the line.

"That's exactly who you better thank," the caller responded, "because apart from the Lord, it never would have happened."

Devotion comes from the heart, delivers faith in action, and leaves the details to God. And the devoted believer makes an impact in every arena of life, including the workplace.

"YOU ARE HERE" MAPS:
DISCOVERING YOUR CALLING

To THIS DAY, *there is a controversy over who first reached the North Pole: Robert Peary or Frederick Cook. Or, for that matter, if either's claim is valid. Although solid proof seems absent, one fact is certain: their explorations more than ninety years ago provide a case study in human motivation.*

Without question, Peary was obsessed. He often claimed himself a victim of "arctic fever," an unaccountable and driving urge to stand on a particular spot of polar ice. For more than a quarter of a century, with at least four different expeditions, Peary jealously stockpiled the necessary inventory of technology, strategy, money, material, and resources to stake a flag—as well as his name—on the North Pole. In his quest, he was fierce, indomitable, creative, single-minded, and often ruthless.

Obsession often drives paranoia, and Peary was a man constantly looking over his shoulder. During one failed expedition in 1898, Peary was experimenting with a new route and was wintering in the Kane Basin of Ellsemere Island, just west of Greenland. On the rumor that another explorer was also attempting an assault on the pole, Peary sought an advantage; in the dead of arctic winter, he traveled more than one hundred miles further north to Fort Conger. Upon arrival, he pulled off his boots and with them, several of his severely frostbitten toes.

Between his various expeditions, Peary, also a journalist, financed his crusade by writing, lecturing, and securing donations from wealthy members of the Peary Arctic Club. Through the donations, Peary was even able to construct a custom ship with a pointed bow designed specifically for penetrating ice: the 184-foot steam vessel, the Roosevelt. *His quest was limitless.*

In contrast, Dr. Frederick Cook's interest in the North Pole was periodic and seemed to be largely fueled as foil: he disliked Peary. Peary had hired Cook as a surgeon and anthropologist for his first expedition in 1891. Ten years later, at his own expense, Cook was part of a relief expedition to treat Peary and his team after another failed attempt. Peary, in poor health, was not a gracious loser; his ill temper offended Cook.

While Peary continued his quest for the Pole, Cook turned to a new venture: the scaling of Alaska's Mount McKinley, whose summit he claimed to have reached in 1906 on his second attempt. About the same time, Peary was launching still another expedition to the Pole; this time his team came within 180 miles of his goal before being forced to return because of dwindling supplies and failing health. In Peary's mind, not one of his expeditions was ever a failure; through each he acquired necessary knowledge for eventual success.

In 1907, Peary planned yet another attempt and began to calculate meticulously what it would take to reach the North Pole: clothes, sleeping quarters, advance teams, dogs, and methods of supply. He would leave nothing to chance; his plans were precise and flawless, the etchings of twenty-five years of firsthand knowledge.

Cook was not as thorough. Hearing of Peary's plan, Cook and a wealthy friend quickly put together an expedition of their own, launched in August 1907. Peary, unaware of Cook's attempt, set off on February 19, 1908.

On April 2, 1909, Peary, his partner, and four Eskimos made the final assault to the North Pole: five days of grueling, nearly nonstop, sleepless march. On April 7, he stood on the ice that he believed to be the North Pole.

Upon his hoped-to-be triumphant return to New York, Peary was greeted with news: Cook's claim, just five days earlier, that he had reached the Pole less than a year earlier—on April 21, 1908. Having gone off-course on his return trip from the Pole, Cook and his crew were forced to winter in an ancient dugout on James Sound, living off the land to survive, thus delaying the news.

Although Cook's claim was generally dismissed as fraudulent, he had accomplished at least part of his objective: to steal the thunder from Peary. A controversy, fanned by rival newspapers supporting each of the explorer's claims, raged for the next five years. After pursuing for nearly half of his life his obsession to be the first to reach the North Pole, Peary never fully received recognition for his effort.

Both of the explorers' lives ended far short of their dreams. Cook, without an anchor of integrity, was later convicted of mail fraud for selling worthless real estate. Peary suffered from bouts of depression. The North Pole, once an arctic *fever racing in his blood, had become in his mind simply another pile of bone-chilling ice. He remarked, "It seems so simple and commonplace."*[1]

What We're Doing—and What We're Meant to Do

Not another buyout. Brad Dunstan (not his real name) stood in the hall-way, shaking his head in disbelief at the latest rumor working its way around the company. Through a series of buyouts and mergers that kept rolling over his department like so many tidal waves, he'd had four different bosses in the past eighteen months. After each restructuring, he had struggled to regain his footing before his staff of twenty-eight design and development professionals lost momentum on their project.

When he'd taken over the department, morale ebbed and flowed between disgruntled and passive. So he had immediately set up one-on-ones with each direct report in which he asked, "What do you like about your job? What do you dislike about your job? What would your ideal job look like?"

He'd listened carefully and then made it his goal to reassign responsibilities accordingly. New goals, new mission, new projects. Then it was time to start all over again: another department to restructure and people to reassign. That accomplished, enter the third new boss under the latest merged regimen.

He couldn't see an end to it. With a master's degree and twenty years' management experience under his belt, Brad wondered: Was this all God had for him to accomplish with his life? Move people around? Reassign responsibilities? Develop models, manuals, and web modules? To what end? Was he wasting his talents? Maybe God wanted to use him to run some nonprofit ministry somewhere. Certainly Dallas had its share of needy ones. Or maybe he should serve on a church staff as a business manager. Or travel around the country speaking, like some of the experts he hired to conduct leadership training sessions. Or maybe go into schools and try to reach youth before they got off track. Or maybe . . .

> For someone unanchored by a higher calling, the marketplace is unsettling, potentially numbing.

He dreaded going home to Carol again with what was becoming a low-grade grumble. How could he tell her the buyout might mean a move? Why should he be this unsettled at this stage in life? How could he ever advise his boys about college and vocation when he couldn't even find his own niche?

Two hours later, Brad flopped down at the dinner table. Disappointed. Defeated. Depressed.

Scan the business page of your local newspaper, and mark the volatility implicit in its vocabulary: *merger, flagship, bench mark, antitrust, empowerment, acid test, comer, takeover, globalism, hired guns, a killing, redline, paradigm shift, watchdog.* Section D, page 1 is not exactly a haven for spineless nouns and passive, weak-kneed verbs. Adjectives bite. Direct objects are aggressively stated. Bullheaded pronouns rule. One might just as well be reading an encyclopedic description for *typhoon*, or the cheat sheets to computer games that spill blood. It's hard not to get swept away.

The business world is nothing if not the fierce reality of continual and aggressive change. And underneath the vocabulary, like blood raging behind skin, flow the torrents of motivation: ambition, obsession, conquest, rivalry, jealousy, and profit. Even in more compassionate companies balanced with soft sides, an edge exists: the necessary blade of movement and mangled progress. You can't escape it.

For someone unanchored by a higher calling, the marketplace is unsettling, potentially numbing. Either like Frederick Cook, he becomes discredited, or like Robert Peary, disillusioned.

Capturing a Sense of Calling

Calling, at its most basic level, is the expression of a higher purpose. In the fierce swirl of the temporary, calling moors us in the eternal. Beyond God, we cannot be moved. Calling informs us, always reminds us: our lives are larger than our puny selves. In the Bible, calling is twofold: God calls each person to himself, to salvation, and God calls each person to his or her work as part of his divine agenda.

When the apostle Paul wrote in Romans 8:28 that each follower of Christ is "called according to his purpose," he was explaining our adoption and unstoppable growth in the family of God. We have been, quite literally, saved. We draw our life from the everlasting life of God. But when God says to Jeremiah, "Before you were born . . . I appointed you as a prophet to the nations" (Jer. 1:5), the calling is to a specific work assignment. God had a job for Jeremiah. Scripture records several instances of God calling people to specific work: Moses, Paul, Isaiah, Nehemiah, Josiah, John the Baptist, Elisha, and Stephen, to name just a few.

Calling, then, is both general and specific. Our calling in life, again in the words of Os Guinness, means that "everything we are, everything we do, and everything we have is invested with a special devotion, dynamism, and direction lived out as a response to His summons and service."[2] Calling encompasses all of what it means to be human. In the words of Mother Teresa, "Many people mistake our work for our vocation. Our vocation is the love of Jesus." And in turn, part of our vocation—and one we are specifically called to by God—is our work.

> When we come to grips with the idea and magnitude of God's calling, we are less tempted to define success as a promotion to the seventeenth floor or a vacation in the Swiss Alps.

The Bible includes many verses that have to do with a calling connected to our work. And fewer than half have anything to do with a full-time Christian vocation; more than half refer to God calling somebody to the marketplace: to cut jewelry, dig ditches, build roads, nurse the sick, take notes as a scribe, play music, shepherd, rule a kingdom. He still calls us to design websites. To decide court cases. To deliver copy machines.

Or counsel criminals. Lieutenant Timme Pearson oversees programs for offenders at the Colorado Women's Correctional Facility; these include addiction recovery programs, family counseling, and Bible studies. With a cadre of volunteers, she works out God's calling to implement lasting change in the prisoners.

A calling to work is the individual tether that connects us to the overarching principle of stewardship: We were created in God's image, and therefore we are expected to manage his resources (talents, skills, gifts) the way God would manage them. That self-management or stewardship becomes true and fulfilling work.

Anchored in eternal reality, we are freed to view our work from a perspective above the swirling change of day-to-day business. But at the same time, we are not "above it all," exempted from, or unchallenged by the everchanging realities of the work world before us, temporary as that work may be. God mandates that we join the fray. We plant eternal seeds in the ground of the every day. Our work involves the implementation of God's agenda in history.

When we come to grips with the idea and magnitude of God's calling, we are less tempted to define success as a promotion to the seventeenth floor or a vacation in the Swiss Alps. In our work, we are called to higher, more attainable realities, and to a deeper fulfillment and sustaining significance.

The Call: Simple and Difficult

Calling is a simple matter: someone calls and someone responds. Ma Bell could tell you that.

God, of course, is the one on the line. And God is, if nothing else, a master communicator: the roar of a thousand voices and a still, quiet whisper. He revels in revelation. If one does not hear the call of God, the problem can be complex, with a range of potential explanations and remedies.

For starters, we may not recognize the voice of God. Quite often, it seems disguised, like the thrown voice of a ventriloquist. God's voice may seem distorted or unclear, fused in the rattle and chaos of our own private worlds. At other times we don't hear God's call because we are expecting either the dramatic or the bizarre.

Such was the case with John Gayle (not his real name), a software engineer in Dallas who stumbled upon a new application for technology in the utilities industry. By day, he consulted with a utility company in Oklahoma City, on-site for weeks at a time, customizing software for the company's applications. By night, he worked on his own software idea. Once he had a prototype completed, he began calling his network of friends for sources of financing. All the while, he worked under great stress, dividing his attention between the Oklahoma City client, who wanted fifty to sixty hours of his time each week, and his family, who wanted him to get his new entrepreneurial venture off the ground so he could stop traveling and be home with them.

Then one day, at the end of a long discussion about the software prototype, John's advisor-friend asked, "So have you thought about asking that key client in Oklahoma City, who already thinks you hung the moon, if he'd be interested in funding your new software venture?"

The question hit him upside the head like a baseball bat. *Indeed, why not?* He got back on the plane to go ask. They were. Deal done.

John's not all that peculiar. The world is rife with hungry salespeople chasing the big fish in the ocean of buyers when God keeps sending them trout in the mountain stream running through their backyard. There's the screenwriter who's hawking her script in Hollywood while the film producer's scouting the local writers group in Galveston. Or the entrepreneur hiring a recruiter to find a general manager for his business while his vice president of operations with the prerequisite experience searches the Internet for job opportunities.

In a fallen world and through fallen hearts, we sometimes are expecting a divine call with bandwidth well above 900 megahertz, crystal-clear. Our confused expectations and the other distortions while listening for God's call are real.

Pearson O'Neil (not his real name) can certainly attest to that. Pearson, forty-two, grew up in a family of preachers, his father pastoring a megachurch and later becoming a denominational leader. Coming out of that background, Pearson assumed that if he were serious about serving God, that meant a full-time Christian vocation. Despite an early failed marriage and a slight learning disability, he struggled through college and seminary. Although it took him longer than most to finish both academic programs, he felt God blessed persistence and so he trudged full-speed ahead. He finally found a church pastorate in Arizona; before long, he was released from that job. Then he moved on to a church in Florida and within two years, he was released from that church also.

His personal life was holding up no better. The success and job satisfaction of his wife, a gifted college professor, only added to his pain. Still together only in name, they and their two children merely went through the motions of day-to-day living.

During the Christmas holidays at a community get-together, Pearson mumbled that he'd like to talk with me (Steve) for a moment. Once we stepped outside, he fell into uncontrollable sobs. Intermittently, he talked about how his personal life, professional life, and family life had cratered. "What's wrong with me?" he asked. "What kind of future can I ever have? Life is over for me."

"Pearson, here's the way I see it," I said. "You've had a tough background, but God has given you gifts. He has to have a place for you. He has a purpose for your life. We have to have the confidence to figure that out."

"But I've failed at everything I've tried to do."

"What are you good at? What are your strengths?"

"I don't know. I hate speaking in front of a group. I just can't do that anymore." As he continued to talk, the pieces fell in place. Had he been a professor, a politician, or a Hollywood performer, he'd certainly have failed as well. He was acting outside his natural skill set.

So together we began sessions to identify his natural, God-given skills and gifts. And in the course of that pursuit, he had to rethink his entire theology. He grew up thinking a husband acted like Archie Bunker and that a person could serve God only in a church.

Where's Pearson O'Neil today? He's a manager at a national retail chain, exercising his gifts of serving people, showing compassion, and taking care of their needs one on one. With a twinkle in his eye and loving every minute, he says that God called him to be a "retail chaplain." And his wife and family agree, even though they are living on less than one-third of the salary they'd grown accustomed to.

> Distortion; misunderstanding; wrong-headed counsel from parents, friends, or colleagues: above all the cacophony of commerce and community, God calls. Our ability to hear that call requires a devotion to God, evidence that we have spent enough time in his presence to be able to recognize his voice from noise that has flooded our lives.

The story of Mike Lunceford's calling follows the same general lines, but with a few unique twists. Like Pearson, Mike had grown up in a Christian home and a great church, so it was only natural that when he went away to college and expressed his desire to serve God in a significant way, college buddies assumed he'd go into the full-time pastorate. Knowing that he wasn't especially talented in speaking, but with natural singing ability and a gifted guitar hand, Mike assumed God would use him in the music ministry. So after completing an undergraduate degree in music, he studied theology for a year. That's when he began to question his career path. *This isn't me. This isn't who I am.*

That realization set him on a path of self-discovery. What jobs had he taken after college? Not part-time church jobs, but jobs in banks. He'd always loved working with numbers. So despite his friends' questioning his passion to serve God and dousing him with guilt about "leaving the ministry," he flip-flopped his world, entered the business track, and became a certified public accountant. He married, had two kids, and moved back to Jackson, Mississippi, to begin working his way through the banking industry.

And his life filled with energy, passion, and connection to God's purpose in the world.

Fast forward to North Carolina, where he took a job with a Big-Six accounting firm for the next few years. Although sure that he was working within his skill set, he grew dissatisfied with his fast-paced lifestyle. So he decided to move back to his roots in Mississippi to enjoy a slower pace that allowed more time with his wife and family. Establishing his own CPA firm there, he has also joined Larry Burkett's ministry, counseling families on biblical financial principles. With a solid family life and a correct theology, Mike has become salt and light in that corner of the world.

As we've watched him discover and live out God's purpose in his life, we've wondered at the irony of well-meaning friends who chided him for "leaving the ministry" in his younger days. Even well-meaning friends and colleagues sometimes serve only to muddy God's message to us.

Distortion; misunderstanding; wrong-headed counsel from parents, friends, or colleagues: above all the cacophony of commerce and community, God calls. Our ability to hear that call requires a devotion to God, evidence that we have spent enough time in his presence to be able to recognize his voice from noise that has flooded our lives. Silence, a sense of inner stillness, surfaces as a rare but necessary commodity in finding our calling.

Four Channels for God's Call

In general, God calls us to our work in four different ways:

- By name.
- By placing an unquenchable desire in a heart.
- By arranging a clear path.
- By preparing an attractive option.

Let's take a look at all four of these models.

By Name

God called Abraham so clearly, so precisely, so unambiguously that there really was only one possible response. "The LORD had said to Abram, 'Leave your country, your people and your father's household and go to the land I will show you'" (Gen. 12:1). Moses had a similar experience in his calling (Exod. 3:1–10). Although Moses didn't respond in eagerness to the call, he didn't doubt that God had called him.

Paul's call was equally dramatic:

> As he neared Damascus on his journey, suddenly a light from heaven flashed around him. He fell to the ground and heard a voice say to him, "Saul, Saul, why do you persecute me?"
>
> "Who are you, Lord?" Saul asked.
>
> "I am Jesus, whom you are persecuting," he replied. "Now get up and go into the city, and you will be told what you must do." (Acts 9:3–6)

Over the next few days God used Ananias to communicate his specific calling to Paul. Others, too, experienced God's call by name: Joshua, Aaron, Ezekiel, Samson, Elijah, Matthew, Peter, James, and John the Baptist.

But since the time of Jesus and the intercessory mission of the Holy Spirit, God rarely calls individuals directly; usually calling comes from a blend of the other three methods.

By Placing an Unquenchable Desire in a Heart

Nehemiah felt such a burning within his being. Close to the top execs, he had access to information. And what he heard troubled him. The walls around Jerusalem lay in rubble. Nehemiah wept, mourned, fasted, and prayed for days. Yes, in his position of power in the palace of King Artaxerxes, he'd heard bad news before. But this news affected him deeply. There was no other explanation to his reaction other than God intended it. The burden he felt was God's undeniable call to a very specific task of rebuilding the wall.

Isaiah, on the other hand, had a wonderful vision. He saw God's holiness and immediately fell on his face with contrition for his own sin. When Isaiah was cleansed and forgiven, God asked who would represent him, and Isaiah volunteered: "Here am I. Send me!" (Isa. 6:8). That heartfelt passion launched the career of one of the major prophets of the Old Testament era.

God still calls people in the same way today: by planting an unquenchable passion in the center of their psyche.

Author Dianna Booher describes just such a passion. At her work, she loses all sense of time and place, completely lost in creating words on paper. Yet her path to this place where she fulfills her God-given passion was a circuitous one. From about the age of twelve, she felt God's tug on her heart to do something significant with her life. But it took her four years to tell anyone about the desire, and another eleven to figure out how to express her commitment.

At age twenty-seven, Dianna found herself responsible for supporting her family. Her husband suffered from mental illness and could no longer work; they had two young children. After teaching school one year, she knew she had no desire to continue down that track. In a counseling session with an educational director at her church, she expressed her lack of enthusiasm for teaching and the counselor asked what Dianna really enjoyed doing. Dianna had never considered pleasure part of making a living. But she remembered a teenage talent for writing, something she had really enjoyed as well. Her counselor encouraged her to explore what careers might match that enjoyment.

That afternoon Dianna drove to the public library and checked out every book she could find on careers in writing: from greeting cards to romance novels to inspirational how-tos. As she pored over her options, a call came inviting her to write a series of Bible study materials for her denomination.

With her husband hospitalized for depression, Dianna tossed and turned for three nights without sleep. She worried about what her future might hold. She turned over the writing offer she'd had. And she remembered her sense of calling as a teenager to serve God.

At three o'clock in the morning, she pulled on her robe and padded into the family room with her Bible. "God, I don't know what you have for me to do with my life, or how I'm going to support this family. I want to become a writer with all my heart, but I don't see how I can make a living. Lord, you've just got to give me an answer—now. I need sleep." A sense of peace fell over her, one she'd never experienced before. *Write.* She said it aloud to herself, closed her Bible, and padded off down the hallway back to bed. And to sleep.

The following morning, she offered her resignation as a teacher, effective three weeks later at mid-term, certain she was on the right path. But the school board rejected her resignation because the district had no other qualified Spanish teachers. So much for clarity of calling—Dianna spent the next four long days perplexed. On the fifth day, she received a note to report to the principal's office during her conference period. "I just got a call from a woman who's moving back here to take care of her mother who's ill," the principal explained. "And she's looking for a teaching job at mid-term or sooner. Spanish."

Thirty-nine books later, Dianna can affirm that when God places a passion in your heart, he has a plan and a purpose.

Ricardo Valencia's passion is children—in twenty-five thousand classrooms in fifty states. He took a position at *USA Today*, where he could work to ignite love for reading and an intense interest in current events. *USA Today* provides a learning guide to challenge students to read short news items, think critically about them, and then discuss their ideas and conclusions.

According to Ricardo, he didn't always follow his passion. First, he chased the dollar as a produce broker. But after reflection on his own growing-up years in a Christian home, his passion to teach kids about this love, compassion, family values, and unwavering faith led him to his calling.

Does the passion hold after all these years? He says, "I wake up and pinch myself each day for the work I am doing. How did I get so lucky? I thank God."

Randi and Kirk Walters understand a similar sense of calling that God implanted in their hearts. Kirk coaches basketball and teaches in an inner-city junior high school in California, while Randi is a licensed clinical social worker specializing in child welfare. They're an intelligent, personable, nice-looking couple who could find a job anywhere. Do they ever go home at night after a church worship service and say to themselves, "Gee, I wish I could do something significant with my life"? No way. They carry a passionate love for the poor in their heart, and they are convinced they have a great deal to learn from people who live in different circumstances. There's no doubt God has called them to their jobs.

By Arranging a Clear Path

Having been called to his career in disgrace, Daniel was among a group of captives taken from his home in the promised land to the capital of a powerful and pagan empire. He rose to serve as a top administrator in Nebuchadnezzar's court. Although King Nebuchadnezzar was one of the cruelest rulers of his day, he became a follower of God through Daniel's influence. Daniel's career and calling spanned four kings and three empires. No doubt, he was called to his place of service as a business administrator.

God called Josiah at an early age: to be exact, while in his mother's womb (2 Kings 22). At the age of eight, he became king of Judah and ruled for the next thirty-one years. God put him on his career track with no input at all.

God, still today, is in the business of calling people by setting out a clear path for them to follow. Bubba Lentz was three years old when he began to accompany his dad to construction sites. Had his dad been a mechanic, Bubba might be a mechanic today. But his father worked in construction, and for more than forty-three years, so has Bubba. No, he wasn't forced into that vocation; He was called. He discovered early on that he had real talents as a builder: He could hammer a two-inch nail into a four-inch-wide board directly above his head faster than most men can pull that same nail from the pouch in their belt. Although he tested the waters once as a salesman in a carpet store, it didn't take him long to discover that he wasn't cut out to push product all day.

So Bubba quickly returned to his calling as builder, and he sees God's confirmation of that calling weekly: In the many projects he's voluntarily built across the country for the Torchbearers of the Capernwray Missionary Fellowship, which operates Bible schools and summer camps. In each new client who shows up unexpectedly when needed the most. And when he's given an opportunity to explain the God-connection when clients comment on the quality of the house he's built for them.

By Preparing an Attractive Option

Elisha's calling became clear when a prophet recruited him (1 Kings 19). He was plowing with his twelve yoke of oxen when all of a sudden, Elijah the prophet came up to him and threw his cloak around him. Elisha saw opportunity in the invitation. He kissed his parents good-bye, slaughtered his oxen, fed his friends, and followed the prophet out into the world. God had placed before him the option of a close mentoring relationship with Elijah, followed by an extraordinary career on his own.

Stephen, the first Christian martyr, also was in the right place at the right time. As the young Jerusalem church grew, the operational details became overwhelming for those sent to preach to the crowds. In Acts 6, we learn that the followers of Christ gathered and chose seven men from among themselves to handle the operational details of the growing church and ministry. Stephen was called out, not only by the disciples at large, but by God himself.

Still today we sometimes "choose" a career option because God has led us through preparatory experiences and then made the career or job option attractive to us. In current lingo, we get an offer we can't refuse.

Lu Dunbar is another case in point. Her experiences in working to raise money for three nonprofit organizations opened her eyes to the need for a new organization. Having talked with a variety of women stewards about giving to charity, she realized that they had a strong need for a safe environment in which to network and learn how to handle finances and giving well. These women were from all walks of life—some single, some married, some professional, and some home executives—but they all faced issues that come with being entrusted with financial resources and affluence. She saw widows who faced the new responsibility of managing resources that once were managed by their husbands. She saw married professionals who struggled with how to work together with their spouses. She saw young single women who lacked experience in dealing with the numerous fund-raisers who were calling with the "perfect cause" for them to support. Such experiences helped Lu realized that God wasn't calling her to leave the fund-raising industry, but to shift her focus. Now she heads an organization that helps women become more confident and competent in investing their treasure, time, and talent for the kingdom.

Larry Wheeler (not his real name) experienced God's path before he understood he was on it. When Larry completed his degree from Ohio University, offers for graduate scholarships came from all directions, including Harvard. But having seen enough of the classroom, he was ready for the board room. He accepted an offer from a large multinational corporation and quickly rose to vice president of a Fortune 50 company. Along with each step up the secular ladder of success, he placed himself in a position for spiritual success as well.

Larry was working at corporate headquarters when he became a follower of Christ. But it was a few years later, when he moved to another location and launched an innovative customer business development division, that he gained a real sense of his calling and how his past had prepared him for the new pursuit. In helping engineer a partnership with his company's largest customer, Larry began to explore the idea of linking business principles with biblical wisdom. Every time he had to make a decision in this highly stressful and competitive environment, he turned to the Bible for practical guidance.

Despite resistance from top executives of both companies, God continued to affirm his approach to issues by granting him positive bottom-line results that silenced his critics. The models of leadership, policies, and procedures Larry established are now being used worldwide by his company—although many people in the organization are unaware the ideas came not from a business book but from the bestseller of all time: the Bible.

God prepared him, provided him options, and prompted his responses all the way.

But for Rich Brown, it wasn't until he gave up his dream to become an eye surgeon that he understood his calling clearly. Unlike Larry Wheeler, who became a believer late in life, Rich grew up in a Christian home and simply assumed from an early age that he would be following God's purpose for his life. After four years of college and four more years of medical school, Rich was ready to begin his residency in ophthalmology. He'd been fascinated by how the eye worked ever since he'd undergone two eye surgeries as a child. To be an eye surgeon was, he felt sure, his calling.

Like all would-be doctors, Rich submitted his list of preferred residency choices. The residency programs submitted their lists of preferred doctors. The two lists didn't match.

Rich was devastated. For a time, he ended up working part-time as a night admissions officer at a mental-health clinic. When the workload was light, he turned his attention to prayer. Through those late-night prayer sessions, he came to the conclusion that his career was in God's hands, even if that meant going into one of his least favorite fields—obstetrics and gynecology. After that decision to trust his calling once again to God, an inexplicable peace came over him.

The next morning, Rich got a call from his father. A doctor at the University of Missouri-Kansas City had been trying to reach him. He needed to talk to Rich about an unexpected opening—a residency in ophthalmology. Today, with thirteen years' experience under his belt, he has seen God confirm that calling in many ways as he has worked with patients, staff, and colleagues.

These people feel blessed to have found their calling and continually receive confirmations of their being in the center of God's plan for their lives. For many people, though, discerning their calling can seem a bit of a crapshoot. The questions are incessant: *How do I know the job I'm doing is the one God has called me to? If I feel burned out from time to time, does that mean I'm not in the will of God?*

And, as far as gifts are concerned, it's always this: Some fit and some don't. And, really, that's all beside the point; I am, after all, nothing more than a janitor. With starving children and nuclear disarmament, what could God possibly care about the work of someone who scrubs floors? God calls prophets and artists and leaders, those with Big Ideas, but a factory worker? What use does God have for a fiberglass bumper?

Calling, in fact, can be elusive in terms of both certainty and purpose. Discovering one's calling, in many cases, happens more by accident than by following a formulaic design.

Sometimes, it comes down to what appear to be random events. Alexander Fleming, a bacteriologist, and C. J. La Touche, a mycologist, had laboratories one floor apart. Both had doors opening up into a common stairwell. Because of a continually jammed window, Fleming kept his door open. La Touche, who lacked a fume hood, did the same. Fleming grew bacteria and viruses; La Touche developed strains of mold.

One week in September 1928, Fleming went on vacation, leaving his door open and discarded petri dishes on a table. The dishes—one of which contained a staphylococcus culture—had not been effectively sanitized. Meanwhile, La Touche continued his work with molds, charging the atmosphere with spores, some of which found their way up the stairs and into Fleming's laboratory. When Fleming returned, he noticed something

> Calling is progressive, and like Moses parting the Red Sea, you often have to get your feet wet first.

unusual: A bacteria-free circle had formed around the staphylococcus culture. A mold had created it. Upon further testing, he discovered that the mold—and its active ingredient, which he named penicillin—prevented the growth of the staphylococcus.

The rest is history. It wasn't a matter of pure dumb luck; nothing could have happened if the individual seekers, operating in close quarters, had not been about their dedicated pursuits. That's the way it often is with calling.

Sometimes you hear God's voice best while humming a tune at work. Discovering a calling is not a matter of sitting in a dark closet, waiting for God to tap you on the shoulder and hand you a highlighted classified ad. Calling is progressive, and like Moses parting the Red Sea, you often have to get your feet wet first.

In whatever way God chooses to call, the adventure begins with our response. And the response continues, rather than ends, throughout a lifetime of commitment to follow that call.

Your Assignment May Change

Another confusing aspect of calling is change. Your calling to any one job or career may be short-term. Jesus worked as a carpenter before he assumed his three-year public ministry. Nehemiah went from COO to a complex project manager; his assignment to rebuild the wall lasted fifty-two days. Amos was a shepherd who became a prophet. David went from shepherd to king.

Scott Stein feels that he has had several short-term assignments directly from God. As he tells it, "As a graduate student in English at the University of New Orleans, I thought I'd arrived at my destination—to be an English professor, having received a teaching assistantship and scholarship, with the blessings of the university faculty. But at the peak of this achievement, God directed my attention to a seminary across town.

"After earning a master's degree from the seminary, I set out to do the only work I believed would give me meaning in life—pastoral ministry. I accepted the fact that *other* people did *other* work, and perhaps they were willing to waste their lives on mundane things such as roofing, office work, or running a business. But I was going to do the *only* work for which I thought God truly smiled—vocational ministry.

"Then after two very successful years as a pastor, the church began a sudden decline, during which the decision was made that I would become a part-time pastor. That decision sent me back into the commonplace world of work. I found a job in a small copy shop (printing and graphics were in my blood because my father had been a printer and my wife was a graphic artist). But I continued to see it as silly.

"After a detour job at a national steakhouse chain, I ended up in a job at a large national children's pizza chain. It was there that God began to show me how to relate to teenagers and to minister to their needs. During this time, I also became aware of W. Edwards Deming's teachings on Total Quality Management, and began to see the parallel of good, profitable business practices and how God asked us to do our work for him: 'Do all things as unto the Lord.' It was rather ironic that while working in a restaurant (what I considered the lowest of the low jobs) and ministering to teens that I first began to understand the biblical foundation from which to understand work and how God leads us to our work, regardless of the type job we do.

"Once again, God moved me from the restaurant job to one in a national copy chain. But by this time, I'd begun to enjoy my work and see it as fulfilling, rather than simply a means to 'real work' as a pastor. With this copy chain, I became a full-time training professional and began to see that my real product was developing people. Now I'm in another assignment that helps me understand why God took me through the paycheck years: my skills are useful and desirable. My calling is teaching and developing people, preparing graphics, and demonstrating teamwork and encouragement to those God brings into my path—at whatever job assignment he's given me."

Whether long- or short-term, calling comes fused with purpose. But sometimes, as with Scott's early years, for the life of you, you just can't see it.

Calling is never a trivial matter. Yet it sometimes may seem that way. From an earthly perspective, the calling to be president is certainly more important than a call to be a ditch digger. The one is responsible for world peace; while the other . . . well, let's not get into that. But from an eternal perspective—which only God has—the callings blend into an overall design: the fusion of God's sovereignty over a world's agenda.

Perspective Provides Purpose

While one nurse may consider emptying bedpans menial, another nurse considers it giving care and comfort to the ill. While one teacher may consider his job confronting irate parents and corralling undisciplined children, another teacher focuses on shaping hundreds of members of the next generation, any one of whom may discover a cure for cancer, lead the nation as president, or give millions of dollars to shelter the homeless. While one stockbroker handles trades all day long, another stockbroker may consider her wisdom the tool God uses to make millions for a philanthropist who will support his work around the world. While one administrative assistant may consider making travel arrangements for her boss a routine task, another assistant may understand her bigger role in helping her manager arrive at his destination rested, refreshed, and ready to contribute valuable ideas in a meeting that will shape a new organization.

In essence, God calls us to a career, a job, or maybe a single task as part of his universal project to build. The Bible, as the revelation of God to humans, allows us to focus on the bigger—or maybe hidden—picture. Not only does purpose turn water into wine, but it also transforms an average stone into a part of a breathtaking cathedral. The Bible provides perspective.

Let's consider two illustrations, admittedly inadequate, but maybe helpful. The first are those intricate, "magic" pictures—those you stare into long and hard enough to eventually see a pattern, a design within the seeming chaos. Because most of us end up with only a headache or eye strain, the illustration has limited appeal. But you get the idea: From unexpected places comes the hint of new vision.

Another illustration, closely connected, is the concept of a mosaic. The advertisement for the movie *The Truman Show* was a remarkable example of the use of mosaic art. When you first look at it, you see a picture of Jim Carrey, the movie's star. But when you look closer—at the individual hues and shadows—you realize the picture is actually composed of several hundred smaller pictures, stills from the movie. These tiny, individual pictures, arranged in a perfect

> Calling is key to God's purpose and our passion as the president, the pastor, or the plumber. Work is not just a matter of what we do, but a concrete reflection of who we are.

order to accomplish the correct blending, color, and detail, work together to form the overall portrait. The stills are both uniquely separate and impeccably united.

That is the picture of calling tied to stewardship: uniquely separate and impeccably cohesive.

Calling is God's laboratory. And in his laboratory, he seeks growth, maturity, productivity, and worship. Because calling involves all of who we are, the process is never supposed to turn static. Calling involves movement and change, the "pressing forward to the high call of God in Christ Jesus."

Calling is key to God's purpose and our passion as the president, the pastor, or the plumber. Work is not just a matter of what we do, but a concrete reflection of who we are.

Richard Bolles, author of *What Color Is Your Parachute?* tells the story of how calling was evidenced by a woman who worked as a checker at a grocery store. Describes Bolles:

> She worked in the days when there were cash registers rather than bar code readers, and she would get a rhythm going on the keys of the cash register when she was ringing stuff up. Then she would challenge herself on how she packed the paper bag with groceries. She gave recipes to shoppers who weren't sure how to cook what they were buying. She kept candy for kids and, with permission from a parent, would give it out. She did the work of a checker, which 10,000 people can do, but she did it in her own unique way. She performed all these different roles under the guise of "just" being a checker. That's a basic way a calling gets or should get traced out: Taking mundane tasks and figuring out how to transfigure them. The story in the Gospels of Jesus going up on the mount and being transfigured before the disciples is to me a picture of what calling is all about. Taking the mundane, offering it to God, and asking Him to transfigure it. It isn't a matter of doing a great work like bringing peace into the world, necessarily; it may well mean being a checker. It's in the sense that there's a uniqueness to the way in which you do the task.[3]

In the eyes of heaven, what matters is not so much the kind of work that you do, but its quality. Author Barbara Glanz insists that our work is our masterpiece and that we should sign it with care.

Jesus, in fact, took great pleasure in reversing the traditional order of recognition, what was worthy of our efforts and what was not with his "the first shall be last and last shall be first" pronouncement (Matt. 19:30). The same is also true of work. For his disciples, he mostly chose those who performed the "lower" forms of work: fishing and collecting taxes. Smelling of fish or filthy lucre, their work eventually took on the effervescence of the divine.

We Work for God; He Works on Us

Our work, then, allows God to go to work on us while we go to work for him. Exodus 31 reveals a very specific calling of a worker by God. Even though God knew exactly the blueprints of the tabernacle—down to the color of yarn and height of the candlesticks—he allowed man the privilege of participating in the work. Read the first five verses of the chapter:

> Then the LORD said to Moses, "See, I have chosen Bezalel son of Uri, the son of Hur, of the tribe of Judah, and I have filled him with the Spirit of God, with skill, ability and knowledge in all kinds of crafts—to make artistic designs for work in gold, silver and bronze, to cut and set stones, to work in wood, and to engage in all kinds of craftsmanship."

God called Bezalel for at least two reasons: his spiritual integrity and his skill. The calling was not simply to be a dry, mechanical execution of God's intended purpose. It was to involve all of who Bezalel was and who God had created him to be. Human skill and divine empowerment—what an amazing combination!

Can you imagine the quality of the work of Bezalel? Working from the blueprints of God himself, on a project dear to his heart—can you picture the concentration, precision, passion, and joy of Bezalel in the execution of skill in his work? Do you think he ran around muttering under his breath, "TGIF"? Most likely he woke up on Mondays, or its Hebrew equivalent, with the largest smile of the week.

While the principle of stewardship is universal, calling, as we can see, is unique. God knows each of us as individual people, intricately and lovingly created. When God calls a person to a particular task or job, he does not forget how he created us: our gifts, passions, temperaments, and experiences. In calling, he blends together all of who we are so that we accomplish, with his grace and Spirit, what he asks us to do. He does not call Reggie White to be an accountant or Tiger Woods to be a professional football player. Calling involves, in a profoundly deep manner, an integration of talents, temperament, tastes, and tasks.

At the risk of stirring controversy, we also could argue that calling, in an indirect fashion, applies to all of humanity. When people call Michael

Jordan, for example, "graceful," they are closer to a deeper truth than they imagined. A leaping, 360-reverse dunk by Jordan—using the gifts, body, and mind God has given him—is truly a work of beauty, a direct reflection of God's intricate, powerful design. The same could be said when Bill Cosby launches a joke or Bill Gates introduces another software package or Celine Dion hits a high C. Maybe without recognizing it as "theological," these people are writing endorsements and accolades for God.

Obstacles to Accepting Your Call

Every follower of Christ who feels called to a job he or she loves will have to struggle against the infection and disease of our culture's self-serving, self-consuming view of work. Even believers who are called to their work will struggle against this tempting viewpoint: "I am doing it all for me. I need to make sure you honor and respect my skill and my accomplishments. I need to make more money than I did last year. I need a promotion. I am the primary customer of satisfaction surrounding this job." Such a struggle ebbs and flows with ego.

A public relations firm in Nashville became a hotbed of seething unsettledness for the two owners and the eight professionals they'd hired during the course of growing their company. As believers, the two owners had surrounded themselves with like-minded individuals to whom they'd "sold the dream" of serving Christian artists and Christian businesses with their creativity: packaging products, developing marketing strategies, creating

> A calling is not always a slam dunk or a flawless note. Calling always will be tested. Obstacles arise, challenges come, pain settles in.

consumer demand, tracking results. But company squabbles began to develop; unrest set in; the owners began to feel as though they'd lost the attention of a few of their employees. After months of agonizing over the situation, the two owners decided to put a tough question to their eight PR specialists: "Would you reconsider your call to be a part of our team? If you feel called to this job, then great. But if not, we encourage you to see where your heart is taking you."

Over the next ten months, four of their PR specialists left. With their departure, additional details of their discontent came to light. Two of the four departing employees had already started their own entrepreneurial ventures "on the side," some with the firm's own key clients. Although the departures created risk with clients, tested relationships with partner firms and long-term employees, and ruffled social relationships among the Nashville crowd, the owners still feel they did the right thing in encouraging their employees to reexamine their calling. Calling is key to contentment—for all involved.

As long as we're human, we'll struggle from time to time in reaffirming God's call. We'll occasionally dream of the "perfect job"—one that gives us the greatest amount of time, freedom, money, power, a different lifestyle, or better schedule. Or the opposite: We feel very settled and happy in our job, and then along comes either an enticing opportunity or an unpleasant challenge that forces us to rethink our calling.

> Calling will endure to fulfillment.

A calling is not always a slam dunk or a flawless note. Calling always will be tested. Obstacles arise, challenges come, pain settles in.

A calling can at times even feel like drudgery. A teacher's aide who feels called to the classroom still may hate to grade test papers. A surgeon who feels called to her medical practice still may dislike rising at five o'clock each morning. A small-business owner may still detest interviewing job applicants.

So when passing through the inevitable emotional ups and downs, how do you know when you've found your calling?

First, you'll have godly friends with the gift of discernment and wisdom to affirm your calling. Young Timothy's spiritual mentor, Paul, affirmed his gift for pastoring and teaching in the church. Another sign of having found your calling will be external results. What you do will be successful, assuming you define success correctly. If, like Kirk Walters, you become a coach, working in your calling doesn't mean you're necessarily going to win every game. But it will probably mean that if you announced at the Parent Teacher Organization meeting that you were going to become a college professor, parents of your student-players would be begging you to reconsider. A third way God confirms a call is through a deep sense of "aha," an inner peace about your job or career decision.

We live in a less-than-perfect world. We struggle through times of doubt and indecision. But times of inner struggle and outward testing will, in the end, affirm or deny the reality of the call. Only the call will be enough to pull us through, to endure the hardships, to reassure us in the knowledge that God himself has asked us to do his work. Calling will endure to fulfillment.

The "Compensation Package" for Your Calling

Writing in Ecclesiastes toward the end of his life, Solomon devoted an entire section to work. He hammered on the theme that a godly person will find meaning, satisfaction, and fulfillment in work: "I know that there is nothing better for men than to be happy and do good while they live. That everyone may eat and drink, and find satisfaction in all his toil—this is the gift of God" (Eccl. 3:12–13). Not everyone finds this sense of meaning in work, only those who are godly. The writer clarified: "To the man who pleases him, God gives wisdom, knowledge and happiness, but to the sinner he gives the task of gathering and storing up wealth to hand it over to the one who pleases God" (Eccl. 2:26). Nonbelievers never have the sense of meaning in their work that followers of Jesus experience.

Knowing that God has assigned your work and cares about its quality—what more compelling reason to get up when the alarm clock sounds each morning? What a sense of intrinsic motivation! A calling provides the perfect antidote to our self-serving, self-consuming view of work.

With calling comes great relief. Understanding your calling will lead to a sense of being vocationally settled. Instead of the endless chases after money, power, title, position, and climbing one step further up the company ladder—to those ever-elusive and sometimes violent steps of satisfaction—calling embeds itself in peace, restfulness, and contentment. Calling tells us no less than that we are doing the very work of God. And what, beside that, is worth pursuing with all our passion? With a sense of calling in our day-to-day work, we are leveraged in eternity, settled in deep fulfillment.

PART IV

LIFE VERY WHOLE—
BRINGING HOME THE BOUNTY

7

EMERGENCY TRAVEL PLANS:
GUARDING YOUR INTEGRITY

THE SEVENTEEN-YEAR-OLD PREGNANT *girl spoke little, if any, English when her husband introduced her to one of America's foremost exploration teams. But for Meriwether Lewis and William Clark, the young Shoshoni Indian was a god-send. A fortuitous discovery during their mission of discovery, she would help pave much of their way across the Continental Divide.*

Sacagawea had been kidnapped around the age of twelve and taken east to what is now North Dakota, where she was sold to a French-Canadian fur trader, Toussaint Charbonneau. She was carrying Charbonneau's child in the winter of 1804–05 when they visited a small, newly built triangular fort that was the temporary home of the Lewis and Clark expedition. The team of roughly fifty explorers was resting for the winter after a rigorous 164-day trip of 1,510 miles up the Missouri River from the Illinois side of the Mississippi River. And they were preparing for the next leg of their journey—the leg that would take them into the Rocky Mountains and through the former homeland of their new-found Indian friend.

Though she spoke haltingly in English, Sacagawea spoke fluently both Shoshoni and Minitari. The explorers realized that her memories of the land and her ability to help negotiate trades with the natives would be invaluable. Of equal, if not greater, value was the symbolism of her mere presence with the troupe. As Clark put it in his journal, "No woman ever accompanies a war party of Indians in this quarter."[1] First impressions would go a long way with the tribes they might encounter, and Sacagawea would serve as a human truce flag.

So Charbonneau, Sacagawea, and their infant son—Jean Baptiste, who was born in February 1805 and soon nicknamed "Pomp" by Lewis because of the way the babe bounced around—joined the team. Sacagawea and Charbonneau acted as interpreters. Pomp served as a symbol of future generations, a source of inspiration, and at times, entertainment.

Up the Missouri River the team traveled, battling the weather, the land, and the animals in their quest for the Pacific Ocean. At one point, in the vicinity of what is now Great Falls, Montana, the team was forced off the water, so they built cottonwood wheels upon which they pushed and pulled their canoes some eighteen miles around a series of five waterfalls.

When the river broke into three forks, Sacagawea knew that she was almost home. It was near the fork that her people had hunted and gathered food. In a scouting expedition, Lewis came upon a spring in the mountains that he called "the most distant fountain"[2] of the Missouri River. Shortly thereafter he found himself standing at a stream that carried its water westward into the Columbia River and on to the Pacific Ocean. Lewis had crossed the Continental Divide.

The explorers soon encountered the Shoshonis. Sacagawea was reunited with a childhood friend who had escaped their kidnappers and a brother, who had risen to the position of tribal chief. Sacagawea helped the team find a guide and trade for horses for their trip through what the Shoshonis called the "formidable mountains."

Surviving a brutal winter, the explorers worked their way through the mountains and toward their goal. On November 7, 1805, Clark wrote of "Great joy in camp we are in View of the Ocian, this great Pacific Octean which we been so long anxious to See [sic]".[3] The expedition still was twenty-five miles upstream on the Columbia, and it's unlikely that the team actually saw the Pacific Ocean. But their renewed hope helped sustain them during a nine-day downpour that brought parts of the Pacific upriver to them.

Finally, 554 days after they began their quest, Lewis and Clark—not to mention Sacagawea, Charbonneau, "Pomp," and the rest of the team—stood in the sands of the Pacific, 4,132 miles from their launch site.

In one sense, their journey had been a failure. President Jefferson had commissioned the expedition in hopes of discovering an easy connection between the Missouri and Columbia rivers that would make for viable trade and transportation routes. Although a more southern route would eventually be identified, Lewis and Clark had laid the groundwork for all future explorers. Their detailed journals proved invaluable in the country's understanding of the land—its people, its resources, and its animals.

Filling Your Sails with the Right Wind

A number of years ago, executives at Merck, a leading pharmaceuticals company, found itself at a difficult crossroads. A company scientist discovered that a veterinary drug his company had developed possibly could be adapted to kill the parasites that cause the horrible disease, River Blindness. The prospect for finding a cure for a disease that causes such terrible suffering would normally be a cause for celebration.

But here was the dilemma: the customers for the drug were the poor of Africa and Latin America, who could not afford to pay for it. The fact that Merck is a publicly held company compounded the issue. The executives, as employees of the owners, had an obligation to return wealth to shareholders by seeking profit. The price tag on the dilemma? It would cost more than $20 million a year simply to transport the drug, if in fact they decided to give it away. Stranded between right and wrong, one brave executive dug back to the founder's intent. George W. Merck had written, "We try never to forget that medicine is for the people, it is not for the profits; the profits will follow. If we remember that, they have never failed to appear."[4] With that statement in mind, the Merck executives decided to develop the drug called Mektazan and give it away to any country asking for it. Doing the right thing didn't affect Merck's status as one of America's leading pharmaceuticals companies.

Other believers in the marketplace have made equally difficult decisions through the decades. In early November 1999, Omni Hotels sent out a press release announcing an initiative that would cost the organization $3 million a year in lost revenues. It's not exactly the type of news most companies want to spread, even those that are privately held like Omni. With this press release, however, Omni was making a statement about its integrity, not its balance sheet.

Omni owner Robert Rowling had reached an undeniable conclusion. Perhaps someone called him on it—a mentor, an employee, a customer. Perhaps he came to the decision on his own through careful self-reflection or time spent with God. Regardless, he realized that Omni's corporate policy was out of line with his personal convictions. So he pulled the plug on adult pay-per-view movies in the chain's 9,100 guest rooms. In addition to the lost revenue, the company would have to spend another $3 million immediately to replace the televisions in the rooms. But as Vice President for Marketing Peter Strebel pointed out, "Not all business decisions should be fiscally driven. We believe that this is the right thing to do."[5]

Howard Hendricks, the noted professor at Dallas Theological Seminary, might say that by making such an unconventional business decision, Rowling was attempting to live "without wax." During the days of the early church, pottery occasionally made it to market with a thin crack in one side. Some potters would fill those cracks with wax, then turn the pot or jar so that its best side faced forward. This led savvy customers to ask if the pots were "without wax." It is from that phrase, Hendricks tells his students, that we get the word *sincere*. So when Paul wrote his friend Timothy and referred to a "sincere faith" (1 Tim. 1:5), he was referring to a "seamless" faith or one "without wax."

> Few things rock a boat more than the strong winds and high waves of turbulent ethical waters.

"Sincere faith" captures the idea behind integrity. Authenticity shoves down the barrier between public life and private secrets and yields a genuine transparency that allows others to see Jesus by looking through us. Integrity encompasses both character and competence—what we are and how we live. It reflects our values, our ethics, our morality, our convictions, and our virtues put into action for anyone—or for no one but God—to see. Such authenticity creates wholeness, completeness, seamlessness.

Paul urged Timothy to stay in Ephesus "so that you may command certain men not to teach false doctrines any longer nor to devote themselves to myths and endless genealogies. These promote controversies rather than God's work—which is by faith" (1 Tim. 1:3–4). Paul knew that some of the men in Ephesus had compromised their integrity and "shipwrecked their faith" (v. 19). "Some have wandered away from these and turned to meaningless talk. They want to be teachers of the law, but they do not know what they are talking about or what they so confidently affirm" (v. 6–7).

It has been said that when you do the right thing, you have the wind at your back. Explorers of the Fourth Frontier might question that. After all, a seamless life of integrity in the work world is far from smooth sailing. Few things rock a boat more than the strong winds and high waves of turbulent ethical waters. But try navigating those storms without the Wind in your sails. The result, more often than not, is "shipwrecked" faith.

Integrity, therefore, is an essential reality of the Fourth Frontier. To get an appropriate handle on integrity, we must understand how it's developed, expect that it will be tested, and learn to recognize its true, lasting value in the marketplace.

Develop It Before You Need to Display It

We can all recall media stories of a child or teen finding a lost wallet full of money and returning the wallet to the owner with the money inside. But as we age, the dilemmas get more difficult.

David Miller's career ladder was leaning against the home of a mortician when he experienced the first memorable test of his foundational integrity. Before he went to work at IBM and before he worked his way into a corner office with a top international investment bank, David painted houses. He and his brother knew a high school teacher in Pennington, New Jersey, who spent summers painting houses and who was willing to train them in the craft. Soon the brothers launched their own business as a means for paying for their college educations.

After painting a couple of homes, the Millers' confidence grew. Although the work was hard, they enjoyed it. They were doing a good job, and they were making money. At least, that's the way it was until they painted the home of the local mortician.

Halfway through the project, the young entrepreneurs ran out of paint, so they went to the paint store to buy more. It was only after they completely finished the job that they realized something was wrong.

"David, get down off that ladder and go look at the other side of the house," his brother ordered.

"What's wrong?"

"Just go look."

"Why?"

"Just go look. At the corners."

Irritated, David backed off the ladder and walked around the corner with his brother at his heels.

"No way. I'm not believing this. Crud. Stupid." He just stood, shaking his head as he surveyed the clearly different shades of green that met in the corners. "When we went back for more, maybe the store sold us the wrong shade."

"Maybe it'll be the same when it dries. It's still wet now."

"It's not gonna look any better ten hours or ten days from now."

"Do you think the owners will notice?"

"Of course they'll notice. Unless they don't come home until after dark. In which case they won't shoot us until tomorrow at dawn."

The store had not sold them the wrong paint. But they learned that different dye lots sometimes result in different colors. It simply was a bad break. Considering the fact that their entire summer profits would be wiped out if they corrected the problem, David and his brother stood in bewildered silence. *Okay, so let's just get the money and leave before maybe he inspects it:* It was a tempting thought, but not one they could entertain seriously.

> We aren't born with or without integrity. It's a character muscle we either develop or ignore. And it's rarely a last-minute decision.

When they explained to the homeowner what had happened, an unasked question—"What are you going to do about it?"—hung in the air as the painters silently prayed that two-tone green might suddenly take life as the latest hip trend for home exteriors.

It didn't happen.

David and Bob Miller had a decision to make, right there on the spot. "So which shade of green do you like the best?" At their own expense, they made it right.

Much like devotion, integrity is a reality that we can control. We aren't born with or without integrity. It's a character muscle we either develop or ignore. And it's rarely a last-minute decision. According to General Norman Schwarzkopf, "The truth of the matter is that you always know the right thing to do. The hard part is doing it."[6]

Recently, in what was called the worst cheating scandal in San Diego State University's history, twenty-five students were caught cheating on a quiz. The class? Business ethics.[7]

Although school's out for professionals on the job, that foundational radar for right and wrong has become more and more distorted by the business definition of ethics: "to stay out of court" often sums up that definition. But "staying out of court" falls short as a definition for followers of Jesus. A true take on integrity starts with the Bible, not the balance sheet or the scales of justice. And even believers have difficulty with their internal radar. For some, the definition of freedom has become synonymous with liberation to do whatever we want. By and large, the marketplace has focused on profit, power, prestige, pleasure, and plenty. Ethics has lost its position on the platform.

Why? Because so few people are willing to do the hard work—and make the hard choices—good ethics requires. The foundation for David Miller's integrity came from his parents, his other relatives, his church, and his participation in programs such as the Boy Scouts; it was evident when he was a teenager painting houses and all along the path to the executive suite. Upon that early foundation, David Miller built a solid structure as he concerned himself with his personal set of morals and values, as he deepened his personal relationship with Christ, as he made himself accountable to like-minded people, and as he passed (and failed) integrity tests along the way.

> Integrity requires discipline. It comes from years of practice or, at the other extreme, years of neglect.

Integrity requires discipline. It comes from years of practice or, at the other extreme, years of neglect. Much like the muscles in the human body, it can be strengthened or it can become flabby, useless, counterproductive. And the most important muscle in the body of integrity is the heart.

The Center of Integrity: The Heart

Proverbs 4:23–27 offers some prudent advice:

> Above all else, guard your heart,
>   for it is the wellspring of life.
> Put away perversity from your mouth;
>   keep corrupt talk far from your lips.
> Let your eyes look straight ahead,
>   fix your gaze directly before you.
> Make level paths for your feet
>   and take only ways that are firm.
> Do not swerve to the right or the left;
>   keep your foot from evil.

Jesus said that "where your treasure is, there your heart will be also" (Luke 12:34). If our treasure is in our self-pride, in our lust, in our greed, our hearts will weaken over time and give in to those sins. If our treasure is in our love for God, in our commitment to his Word, and in our faith in his promises, then over time our hearts will grow stronger.

Strength in integrity, by itself, doesn't guarantee success, but it does put us in a position to deal appropriately with the inevitable tests of our faith. For followers of Christ, this strength is rooted in a relationship with Jesus and on convictions that we develop through a devotion to the Way. The words of the prophet Micah are apt here:

> He has showed you, O man, what is good.
>> And what does the LORD require of you?
> To act justly and to love mercy
>> and to walk humbly with your God. (Mic. 6:8)

When weight lifters train on free weights in a gym, they generally work in groups of at least two. In addition to the safety of having a spotter while bench-pressing the weight of a small car, the athletes feed off the encouragement of a partner. Likewise, our integrity is shaped not only by our personal disciplines, but also by the company we keep. In a spiritual sense, either we seek aid from the Holy Spirit or we accept distractions from Satan. In an earthly sense, the people who most influence our daily lives either build us up or tear us down.

Our integrity is shaped not only by our personal disciplines, but also by the company we keep.

Scripture makes clear the dangers of associating too closely with people who lack godly integrity. A quick tour of Proverbs turns up some relevant examples:

> My son, if sinners entice you,
>> do not give in to them.
> If they say, "Come along with us;
>> let's lie in wait for someone's blood,
>> let's waylay some harmless soul;

let's swallow them alive, like the grave,
and whole, like those who go down to the pit;
we will get all sorts of valuable things
and fill our houses with plunder;
throw in your lot with us,
and we will share a common purse"—
my son, do not go along with them,
do not set foot on their paths;
for their feet rush into sin,
they are swift to shed blood.
How useless to spread a net
in full view of all the birds!
These men lie in wait for their own blood;
they waylay only themselves!
Such is the end of all who go after ill-gotten gain;
it takes away the lives of those who get it. (Prov. 1:10–19)

Thus you will walk in the ways of good men
and keep to the paths of the righteous. (Prov. 2:20)

He who walks with the wise grows wise,
but a companion of fools suffers harm. (Prov. 13:20)

It is unrealistic, not to mention unbiblical, to avoid all contact with unbelievers: to hire only believers, to work only for believers, to buy from or sell to only believers. God commands us to go into the world of unbelievers so we can be salt and light for those who need to find him. But without question, the thinking of the people around us will help shape our integrity. It's up to us to walk "with the wise" when we face morally questionable situations. Good character keeps good company.

David Miller learned this "walk with the wise" principle of accountability and counsel with his first boss at IBM, who made clear his ethical expectations both in words and in practice. That boss gave Miller three basic rules: be honest; be on time; be a team player.

> It is unrealistic, not to mention unbiblical, to avoid all contact with unbelievers: to hire only believers, to work only for believers, to buy from or sell to only believers.

When Miller moved on to Midland Bank in London, he watched as his boss dealt with a senior manager who had covered up the truth. It wasn't a life-or-death issue, but his boss dismissed the senior manager. "Some people thought that was harsh," Miller reflects. "But I remember thinking: *that sets a tone. That tells me what's important to him—honesty and integrity.*"

Miller eventually felt a call to leave investment banking to study social ethics at Princeton Theological Seminary, but such work-life experiences provided him the foundation for his next career: helping business leaders, academicians, and clergy better integrate their faith and their work. Along with William Pollard, chairman and CEO of ServiceMaster, he cofounded the Avodah Institute as a means for implementing this vision.

> The development of integrity: it's founded on a good heart. It's based on behavior. It's built over time.

The development of integrity: it's founded on a good heart. It's based on behavior. It's built over time.

Expect Your Integrity to Be Tested

David Miller spoke German, but the German businessman wasn't using words to express his initial thoughts regarding an issue Miller had raised. In fact, he wasn't speaking at all. As the German executive reflected on Miller's suggestion, it was the businessman's facial expression that delivered an unmistakable message: *Are you guys from Mars?*

Miller was a partner in a private investment bank that handled cross-border mergers and acquisitions, investment management, and relatively small stage-two capital-investment projects. One such project was a company in Germany. After purchasing a 49-percent share of the company, Miller's firm began to uncover some disturbing details about its business practices. For one thing, the majority owner was running a variety of personal expenses—everything from cars to tuition for his children's private school educations—through the business. Almost none could be classified legitimately as a business expense. Furthermore, the owner habitually paid kickbacks to and received kickbacks from various providers of material resources.

Miller's investment bank insisted that an accounting firm come in to examine the books. The audit team discovered a peculiar line item. Loosely translated, the line item was for "nondeductible business expenses." In Germany, Miller discovered, this line item was the traditional, and legal, home for a company's kickbacks. It allowed the company to track the expense without acknowledging the recipient. This, of course, made the money tax-free income for the recipient. This procedure was legal, but it served to disguise questionable users of company assets. Miller could have taken a "when in Rome, do as the Romans do" approach, justifying the pay-offs in his head as administrative or brokering fees. But in his heart, he knew these payments crossed the line. Even if they were acceptable in that particular culture, Miller and his team saw them as wrong.

Caught in a quandary, Miller consulted his wife, who taught courses on practical legal ethics. He met with his partners. He talked to auditors. He looked high and low for a creative way to solve the dilemma without making a goal-line stand. Then after coming up with a plan, he still he had to confront the majority owner about the issue and his proposal. And that's when he and his partners got the are-you-from-Mars look. The owner couldn't understand why his foreign investors would object to such a routine business practice. To change the practice would cost him and his investors money: a lose-lose situation. Only because he needed the investors, the German business owner reluctantly agreed to phase out the practice over a period of several months. In the short term, the business lost clients and money as a result of the "no kickbacks" policy.

Miller and his partners, meanwhile, felt an obligation to advise their outside investors that they had some ethical concerns with this particular business venture. And in the long term, Miller's group sold its own interest at a considerable financial loss.

For most of us, when we spend time with other believers in our holy huddles, the temptations are far less intense (although still present). Integrity faces its greatest tests when we are detached from our Christ-centered subculture. People who don't share our values, those who live by a different code, test us in our work environment. They see nothing wrong with cooking the books. A lie is simply a means to a justifiable end. A sexual tryst while on a business trip is simply no big deal. Again, since it is impractical and unbiblical to live totally outside of culture, we must expect our integrity to be tested.

We handle these tests through faith. It took great faith, for instance, for Shadrach, Meshach, and Abednego to face death in a furnace by defying Nebuchadnezzar's order to bow down to his golden image. It took great faith for Daniel to risk death in the lions' den rather than give up his prayer time with the Lord. And it took faith for Larry Langdon to risk unemployment by standing up to the unethical practices of a company vice president.

As a corporate tax attorney for a Fortune 500 company, Langdon had plenty of opportunities to shade the truth or hide questionable business decisions. When he realized a vice president at a company he represented was about to execute an illegal sale, he threatened to ensure that the man went to jail if he pursued the deal. It was a tremendous risk. But the VP didn't fire Langdon. And when Langdon later left to take another job, few people expressed a deeper appreciation for his work than did that particular vice president. For Langdon, the possible consequences were far less severe than they were for Daniel or his friends—he might lose only his job, not his life—but he was willing to face them nonetheless.

> In facing tests of integrity, we can react one of two ways. First, we either pass or fail the test. Second, either we grow stronger from that success or failure or it adds to our character flab.

"A walk of integrity has an initial cost," Langdon says. "But ultimately, people see the wisdom of doing things the right way."

In facing tests of integrity, we can react one of two ways. First, either we pass or fail the test. Second, either we grow stronger from that success or failure or it adds to our character flab.

Daniel's life was one of constant testing in one of the most ungodly environments in history, ancient Babylon. He could have taken the easy way out. He could have eaten the pagan diet. He could have denied his God. ("I'm only doing it to go along, God; you know how I *really* feel.") He could have blended into the culture of his captors. But he chose to stand firm on his convictions. In addition to his devotion to God, or perhaps because of it, Daniel practiced proactive integrity. He understood where he was—the culture, the people—and he understood the tests he would likely face. So when a pop quiz came, he'd done his homework.

The postmodern worldview that pervades the New Economy places all followers of Christ in a modern Babylon. In an age of relative reasoning, it's as important as ever to anticipate when, where, and how an integrity based upon absolutes might face a trial.

For many followers of Christ, breakdowns in integrity occur as a result of ethical "instrument lock," the tendency pilots must fight when shepherding an aircraft during a flight. Their inclination often is to focus primarily on a few select instruments rather than to consistently scan the entire board. The results can be deadly.

So, too, followers of Christ can slip into the deadly habit of focusing on their favorite moral standards. For example, people who are sexually pure can lessen the impact of their witness by being lazy in their work habits. Avoiding instru-

> Followers of Christ can slip into the deadly habit of focusing on their favorite moral standards.

ment lock means constantly scanning the environment to make sure other gauges on our "integrity board"—our truthfulness, our dealings with money, our sexual purity, our devotion to God, our commitment to others, our ability to forgive and be forgiven, our compassion—aren't signaling our downfall.

Prove the Integrity Payoff

As a candidate for a top position with Midland Bank in London, David Miller had two strikes against him: first, he would be the youngest director in the organization. Second, he was a foreigner. This young American had plenty of potential, but could he really handle that much responsibility and all the challenges that came with the job? The CEO reflected on these questions as he scanned Miller's résumé for the umpteenth time. His eyes fell on a particular notation about Miller's background: Eagle Scout. For the CEO, who also had been an Eagle Scout, that gold star broke the tie. That distinction told him nothing about Miller's competencies as a senior executive, but volumes about his integrity.

The CEO hired Miller as director of the bank's global custody and securities services division, which included approximately five hundred people and responsibility for client assets of approximately $150 billion, primarily for institutional clients. His first task: rebuild the division. The CEO had started the job, and Miller's role was to make it happen and see it through to completion.

Although Midland Bank (today part of HSBC Holdings) had a long, rich tradition, the division Miller took over was losing clients right and left. Having stopped investing in its people and new technology, the division now was paying the price. And his boss and the board counted on Miller to turn things around.

Shortly after he was hired, Miller paid a visit to two of the division's biggest clients. One was in Germany, the other in Switzerland. Together they accounted for 25 percent of the division's revenues. Both had sent Midland letters of termination. Fed up with poor quality of service, they planned to take their business to competitors offering better and newer services.

Both meetings were conducted in Germany, and David Miller's clients gave him an earful of all the things wrong with the current—soon to be for-mer—relationship. David took it all in. Then he explained why he'd been hired, what the bank hoped to change in the coming years with the new management team that had been assembled, and what he hoped to accom-plish personally as a manager. His management philosophy, as he outlined it to the wavering clients, hinged on three basic principles: integrity, team-work, and ownership.

"I understand," David told them, "if your letters of termination still stand. But I have one last request: Give us six more months, and we'll turn this thing around."

Amazingly, both clients said yes. He promised to call them each week to talk through any outstanding issues. And six months later, neither was interested in leaving the bank. David believes he was able to sell them on an extension for three reasons: he listened to their concerns. He didn't offer 101 excuses. They bought into his management philosophy built on integrity, teamwork, and ownership.

Of the three, Miller is convinced the third was the most important. Without some signal of personal and institutional integrity, nothing else would have mattered.

But not everyone understands the value of integrity—or has the courage to stand the test of integrity when the wind blows the opposite way. That was the case with a fourth-generation manufacturing company. In its par-ticular industry, rollups were rife. And of course, in a quick-consolidation market, all the kingpin players had to decide if they intended to buy or sell.

The manufacturing company, our consulting client, decided to buy companies and quickly identified several candidates for acquisition.

We were leading the strategy meeting for the executive team to determine its plans for the next year as the team members started to acquire and merge these companies into their culture. During the course of that meeting, the CFO turned to the president and said, "I don't think I've got a balance here that I can take to the bank to get these acquisitions done."

Before the president could respond, a senior vice president, who'd been with the company only six months, spoke up, "Well, why don't we just doctor the books?"

"What did you say?" the chairman asked.

All heads turned in their direction.

"Look," the new VP continued, "we all know that there's a lot of leeway when it comes to putting together a balance sheet. And we know what we can and can't afford to buy. So why not just move around the numbers so that our balance sheet will prove what it needs to prove so that when we go to the bank, we can get this acquisition done?"

"Well," the CEO said hesitantly, "I don't know about that."

"Jason," the chairman cut in again, "that might have worked where you came from, but we don't do that stuff here."

"How come? That's what everybody else does. Why not?"

The chairman's eyes locked on those of the new VP and held for a long moment. "Because it's wrong."

End of conversation.

But it started a great new conversation among the executive team members over the course of the next year. Without "moving the numbers around" on the balance sheet, they decided to sell a few divisions to get the cash to post some real assets to make the acquisitions happen.

Not only did the deals work, but also integrity worked—through the courage and influence of one person. Granted, he was one person in a position of power, but that single voice of integrity steered the ship.

The deep waters can be much more difficult to navigate, however, when the person of integrity stands lower in the hierarchy—difficult, but not impossible.

Serving in the military as a middle manager in inventory and supply, Rich Grimm's boss called him into his office to discuss what he called a "dilemma": "Look, it's a mess. I need you to do the paperwork to cover me on this inventory problem. Do you understand?"

Rich swallowed hard. He understood all too well.

His boss continued, "I made some mistakes, see? And I've already got two strikes against me going into this. If you don't cover for me, I'm going to be kicked out—out of the military altogether. You get the picture?"

Rich nodded, then left his boss's office to figure out how to dig his way through the tunnel. As a recent follower of Christ, he had a short supply of experience on such moral issues and a shorter supply still of Christian friends to call on for counsel. But he did recall the story of Joseph and his appeal to his boss when asked to do something wrong. After the loss of a couple nights' sleep and armed with the only biblical example he understood at the time, Rich returned to the boss's office.

> Despite recent trends and regardless of whether Wall Street salutes, most people in the modern work world have a vested interest in long-term success and stability. People of faith, however, should have an even deeper sense of what long term means. Eternity lends perspective to the meaning and practice of integrity.

"Look, I've been thinking over what you asked me to do. And I can't do it. I'm a new Christian, and I don't know a lot about the Bible yet, but I do understand enough to know what you're asking me to do is wrong."

"Don't go preaching to me," his boss began to yell.

"I'm not preaching, I'm just saying, let's try to figure out another way."

"Ain't no other way. It's too complicated and it's too late," his boss snapped.

"It's never too late for the truth."

"And what does that Bible of yours say about loyalty, huh?"

"Loyalty's not about lying."

"I'm not asking. I'm *ordering* you to sign that paperwork and turn it in."

"I can't." Rich paused to screw up his courage a notch. "Look, let's just tell it like it is. Straight. I'll help you. We'll put together the details so they'll understand it was just a mistake."

And he strode out of his boss's office to do just that. After much thought, he put together a report that explained the reasoning behind his boss's misjudgment, and then focused on their plans to move forward and correct the problem.

The upshot: The boss kept his job. Rich kept his integrity.

Integrity make sense—but sometimes only to those with a long-term frame of reference.

How Eternity Affects Decision-Making

The New Economy drives decisions powered by the engine of technology. And that engine threatens to spin us—sometimes out of control—at a pace unparalleled in history. Strategic plans that once might span a decade into the future now might focus on only the next six months. The shelf life of a new idea isn't much longer than the catch of the day at Pike Place Fish Market in Seattle.

Long-term vision is the loose cog in this ever-spinning model. Perspective for the long term overrides short-term results. Despite recent trends and regardless of whether Wall Street salutes, most people in the modern work world have a vested interest in long-term success and stability. People of faith, however, should have an even deeper sense of what *long term* means. Eternity lends perspective to the meaning and practice of integrity.

> It takes faith to trust God's sovereignty, holding on to hope where others fear failure or dwell in despair.

But we also know from experience—ours and that of others—that doing what's right doesn't always pay off in dollars. In fact, it can cost—big time. The list of martyrs is too long for debate. If other people's experience doesn't demonstrate the cost of integrity, however, examine the events of your own diary: people die. Jobs end. Clients walk away. Companies go bankrupt—all because one person's integrity might compel him or her to choose right over wrong.

It takes faith to trust God to take care of us even if we're fired or suffer adverse physical or mental circumstances for a morally right decision. It takes faith to affirm that such adversity builds character. It takes faith to focus on the eternal, not just the temporary. It takes faith to trust God's sovereignty, holding on to hope where others fear failure or dwell in despair.

When David Miller and his brother spent their own time and money to repaint a mortician's home, they feared the demise of their new little enterprise. Unlike painters with years of experience, they hadn't built such mistakes into their business plan or overhead. But impressed with the finished job—and their integrity—the mortician became their best source for customer referrals. They recouped their short-term financial losses with new business.

David Miller experienced the value of trust built on integrity in a working relationship, an understanding that served him well throughout his career. At Midland Bank, David made it a practice to join people on his staff twice a month for lunch. During these forums, he talked about tennis, his wife, his church. In short, he told them about who he was. He looked for similar opportunities to be up-front about his core beliefs with clients, vendors, and partners. He didn't have to hand out gospel tracts to establish some basic understanding of his faith.

And David got results. For starters, his openness allowed other believers to feel free about expressing their faith in the corporate environment. Second, it served as a preventive measure; as David puts it, "If you're in the dirty-tricks business, you go to someone who has a reputation for doing dirty tricks." Through his words and with his actions, Miller sent a message about the things he would and would not tolerate.

The Old Testament's Daniel, by constantly demonstrating integrity in the face of harsh consequences, sent out similar messages. Daniel's integrity won him respect, honor, and status in the most godless land—ancient Babylon. When the pagan kings could find answers nowhere else, they turned to Daniel. When those kings looked for someone they truly could trust, they turned to Daniel.

Daniel was skilled in his vocation and honest in his work. When King Darius wanted to put an end to corruption among his managers, he assigned Daniel to oversee them. And "Daniel so distinguished himself among the administrators and the satraps by his exceptional qualities that the king planned to set him over the whole kingdom" (Dan. 6:3). When jealous colleagues searched for reasons to bring Daniel down, "they could find no corruption in him, because he was trustworthy and neither corrupt nor negligent" (Dan. 6:4).

For Daniel—and for David Miller, the Merck executives, Rich Grimm, Larry Langdon, and our consulting client who wanted to consolidate—

integrity paid off because it developed a reputation and a trust that generated earthly success.

But there's another reward: If integrity comes from a life with Christ, it doesn't have to be perfect. People make mistakes, either willfully because they lose their focus on Christ or inadvertently because they exercise poor judgment. Integrity grounded in faith allows us to understand our imperfections and to be vigilant in overcoming them. And when that vigilance falls short, we see our mistakes for what they are, learn from them, and move on, accepting grace and forgiveness as God's gifts on those occasions.

Thus the payoff for a life of integrity can be a greater integrity—a greater wholeness. Unlike the ancient potters, our cracks are filled with wax, but they appear seamless again by the redemptive blood of Christ.

SHIPSHAPE ATTITUDES
PRACTICING STEWARDSHIP

ON THE MORNING of June 2, 1953, the citizens of Britain celebrated. Hope, they believed, had returned; a glorious future—matched only by the brilliance of the past—was dawning. Forget about the slow and painful dissolution of the British Empire and the ghost of austerity that had plagued the nation since World War II. Britain once again was on the rise. It was a "new Elizabethan age," as the newspapers had coyly coined it.

In the early edition of the London Times, two stories intersected on the front page: the coronation of Queen Elizabeth and the conquering of Mount Everest by a British team of mountaineers. Separately, grand ascensions; together, an undeniable foretelling of the resurgence of the empire. Anyone who could read between the lines could see the word destiny. It simply had to be so.

As citizens lined the streets of London in anticipation of the coronation procession, they passed along the news: two men from a British expedition— Edmund Hilary, a rangy New Zealander, and Tenzig Norgay, a highly skilled Tibetan Sherpa mountaineer—had become the first men to stand on top of the world's tallest mountain. Scaling the south side of the peak, they had managed to conquer the last barrier, a formidable ridge of nearly forty feet with virtually no holds, to stagger the remaining few feet to the summit, shaped like a "rounded snow cone." At 29,028 feet, they felt more exhaustion than exhilaration.

Now, with a new Elizabeth about to rise to the throne, an entire nation was buoyant, giddy with anticipation. Once again, Britain would ascend to the summit of power and influence. Forty years after the event, the reporter who broke the story for the Times wrote:

Coronation Day, June 2, 1953, was to be a day of symbolic hope and rejoicing, in which all the British patriotic loyalties would find a supreme moment of expression: and, marvel of marvels, on that very day there arrived news from distant places—from the Frontiers of the old Empire, in fact—that a British team of mountaineers . . . had reached the supreme remaining earthly objective of exploration and adventure, the top of the world.[1]

One hundred and one years after Everest had been named the world's tallest mountain— following fifteen failed expeditions to rise to the summit, resulting in twenty-four lost lives—the last frontier on the planet had finally been penetrated. By the British. In the name of a new queen, two men stood on the pinnacle, the stewards of an old guard and a new promise.

The Power of Perspective

Carlos is a scalper, a local who thrives in the pits, trading in ten-year Treasury notes. In his blood pumps the scarlet soup of risk, fear, conquest, exaltation, chaos, and control. He lives for the moment—that precise moment—to sell contracts at their highest possible value. Sometimes, it's a matter of seconds, split. Ask Carlos what he works for, and he will tell you: "To make a killing."

Tseuko sells life insurance (term, variable, and universal), car insurance (with property and bodily injury liabilities), and health insurance (with and without riders). On each sale, she makes a straight commission. Ask Tseuko what she works for, and she responds: "To make a living."

Buster is a brickmaker. Forty hours a week—more when interest rates are low and housing starts are up—he battles fierce heat and terrible fumes, pulling out tray after tray of heated clay from a fiery kiln. The boredom nearly kills him. Ask Buster what he works for, and he shrugs and says: "To make a buck."

Susan is a senator; she is wise and photogenic and has learned the ropes. She loves the adrenaline of debate, the reward of accomplishment, the warm fever of ideology. During her better moments, she believes she is making a difference. She has been trained not to tell you about her lesser moments. Ask Susan what she works for and, if you are not with the press, she says, "To make my mark."

For at least eight hours a day, forty hours a week, two thousand hours a year, and one hundred thousand hours a lifetime, nearly every one of us works. By comparison, even death and taxes seem less certain. One would think that, given its enormous grip on each of our lives, work would form a fist of significance, a handshake of common destiny.

Yet the reality is less convincing. Instead of doing work as our destiny, a calling from God, we force our jobs to work for us; our work, we are led to believe, must make something happen outside of its own inherent value. And in an effort to make that something else happen, we, like a manic clown with balloons, twist motivation into strange and entertaining shapes.

> Bees, bears, and beavers work to survive; people work to manage God's assets.

For many people, work is—or at least becomes—a means to something else, a perceived greater reality. Frankly, many of us see work as a sort of cosmic arcade game where we line up the hours and shoot between blindfolded eyes. Sheer repetition dulls us to the inherent emptiness inflicted on our spirit.

We kill time. We lose perspective. Boredom or addiction creeps in. Author Frederick Buechner writes:

> The world is full of people who in one way or another are by and large merely "getting through" their lives, who are killing their time, who are living so much on the surface of things and are so bad at hearing each other and seeing each other that it is little wonder that one life seems enough. . . . There are lots of people who get into the habit of thinking of their time as not so much an end in itself, a time to be lived and loved and filled full for its own sake, but more as just a kind of way-station on the road to somewhere else, to a better job or the next vacation or whatever, and all the interim time that remains to be killed starts looming up like a great mountain that has to be climbed, so that if there were a little button somewhere that we could push to make it disappear all at once, I am not sure how many of us would have the strength not to push it.[2]

God, as the first worker, did not introduce such an attitude about his work. He worked for six days, with light and atoms and dirt and fire and water, the elemental, and he was satisfied. He did not wish to make a killing or a living or a buck or a mark. He worked and, stepping back from the results, saw that it was good. To drive home the point, he repeated himself. Other than the work itself, God did not need to manufacture a reason for working.

In his image and after his model, God created man, in part, to work: "The LORD God took the man and put him in the Garden of Eden to work it and take care of it" (Gen. 2:15). As we mentioned in chapter 2, even before the realities of family, government, and collective worship, God's first assignment to mankind was this: work. Uncorrupted by the perversions of sin and death, work had to be good—very good. An ideal as high as God is wide, work was no less than the sharing of divine privilege. God asked that we work as he did so that his work, creation, would be cared for.

Robert R. Ellis, writing in the *Southwestern Journal of Theology*, summarized three simple and magnificent truths from Genesis 1:26–30:

- God created, and therefore he owns.
- We manage resources that God owns.
- We were created in God's image, and therefore we are expected to manage resources the way God would manage them.[3]

The fundamental idea of work is stewardship—the task of protecting and adding value to all the assets God has put under our care. Through our work, God asks us to care for his creation. Because we are created in his image, work is in fact one of the defining activities that separate us from other creatures. Bees, bears, and beavers work to survive; people work to manage God's assets.

Work, then, is a big idea and no small matter. In the name of the King, we serve as stewards of all we see.

But we don't live in the Garden anymore. Under the company logo, the return address does not read 777 Paradise Avenue. The real world of work, if one tells the truth, resembles a closed maze more than it does an open invitation. Given the cold, cutting-steel edge of words like *downsizing, bottom line, restructuring, diluted share,* and *brand marketing,* the concept of stewardship seems an antiquated, bloodless dream tucked in the floor joists of some company mailroom on the planet of Gee Whiz. Try saying this at a Chamber of Commerce awards banquet: *Steward.* You might, if you are lucky, get a glass of wine.

In the world of real business—with its brutal competition, refined greed, calculated lust, and adrenaline aggression—*stewardship* is a foreign word. You might just as well be back in the third grade, whispering French to the playground bully. Business is fueled by the idea of ownership: stock options, takeovers, profits, acquisitions, and Fortune 500 reputations. At the very least, you must own a piece of the action. To possess, own, control, manipulate—these are the blood-red staples of corporate Darwinism. Only the strong and powerful survive.

As followers of Christ stuck in grinding, workaday worlds, no one has to remind us of the reality of sin. At work, we always can stumble into the pitfalls of the Fall. Is it any wonder, given the hostile ignorance of the marketplace, that God's intention for work—stewardship—rarely happens? And can we please be excused—thank you all the same—if we "pass" on the ethereal idea of work as care taking, and cut our teeth on something more substantial? A 401(k), for example, or a promotion, or a vacation in the Alps, or a practiced signature on the stacks of monthly bills?

If we are brutally honest, we might say that stewardship sounds like a nice idea if you happen to live in some kind of paradise. But for the rest of us, those who live somewhere east of Eden, work is slightly less noble. At best, we are left to figure out how to make work, in some smaller way, work. Stewardship at work? Work as a steward?

For William Pollard, the signals set up an apparent conflict, as did the name of the company: ServiceMaster. Pollard was being recruited for a job, but the question soon became just what kind of a job. It had been made clear to Pollard, who wanted to leave his role as senior vice president of a college, that should he take a position at ServiceMaster, he might eventually be considered for its CEO. That idea intrigued Pollard. During what he believed would be his last interview for the job, Pollard asked a series of leading questions: just what would be needed to become CEO? At the time, he believed his curiosity natural. But quite abruptly in the middle of the interview, Ken Hansen, then the company CEO, stood up and showed him to the door: "Thanks for your time." His voice communicated the opposite.

Later, Hansen called Pollard for a breakfast meeting. Over a waffle and a cup of coffee, Hansen asked, "Bill, do you want to know why I cut short the last interview?"

Pollard answered, "Sure, I'd like to know."

"If you want to come to ServiceMaster and contribute, you have a wonderful opportunity. If you're coming for a particular position or title or the recognition, then just forget it."

At that moment, Pollard knew ServiceMaster wasn't "business as usual." He also decided this was a company he wanted to work for. He convinced Hansen that he was right for the job, and his contributions, not his selfish ambitions, eventually earned him the CEO title. He currently is chairman and CEO. But lots happened in between.

God as Owner: A Matter of Perspective

For centuries, they were simply mysterious lines on a desolate plain of a Peruvian desert. Although no one knew exactly why they were there, it was clear how they got there. The Nascans, an ancient culture existing from about A.D. 1000 to 1500, had "drawn" them. The Peruvian desert is covered by pebbles containing ferrous oxide, which, over centuries of exposure to the sun, turn a dark patina. With the gravel removed, the soil underneath creates a stark contrast. From a distance, the markings look like a design on a prehistoric Etch-a-Sketch. Maybe, one theory went, the Nascans just got bored.

In 1939, the first planes flew over the Peruvian desert. From their aerial perspective, the researchers were stunned at what they saw: not just random and indiscriminate lines, but massive drawings: a spider (forty-six meters long), a monkey (fifty meters), a guano bird (280 meters), a lizard (180 meters), a hummingbird (fifty meters), a killer whale (sixty-five meters), and—the largest of them all—a pelican (285 meters). These ancient desert drawings were amazingly accurate. The spider, for example, contained one appendage significantly longer than the other, which, in reality, contains a reproductive organ. Each drawing was a work of art and mystery, but for centuries these wavy streaks were mistaken for random lines in a desert.

What was missing earlier, of course, was a proper perspective.

The overwhelming reality of the book of Ecclesiastes is its persistent perspective: Under the sun, everything is meaningless, like disconnected and random lines in a desert. Nothing, in the end, makes any sense.

> My heart took delight in all my work,
> and this was the reward for all my labor.

> Yet when I surveyed all that my hands had done
>> and what I had toiled to achieve,
> everything was meaningless,
>> a chasing after the wind;
> nothing was gained under the sun. (Eccl. 2:10–11)

When it comes to our work, stewardship offers a new perspective. We no longer work "under the sun," but view life from *above* the sun—from God's perspective. The eternal, not the temporal. What was once random and disconnected can finally be seen for what it is: great designs of art and accuracy.

What we do matters. Eternally. Even in a fallen world. Even in a company focused on bottom lines. Even on a factory line of numbing repetition. Even at home doing dishes and dirty laundry. Even in the classroom grading 129 essays under the sun. After the Fall, God's mandate and purpose for work did not change. It simply became more difficult, inevitably intertwined with toil, pain, and opposition: the florist with thorns. The farmer with cockleburs. The engineer with seismic faults. The dentist with cavities. The lawyer with legal loopholes. The programmer with coding errors. The banker with risk. The CEO with entropy. Still we are called to be stewards.

> When fully first realized, the concept of stewardship can take the wind out of most inflated sails.

At first, the realization of our call to stewardship is humbling: we own nothing, God owns everything. Not just the split-level home on a tidy half-acre of prime suburban property, but also our bank account, our family, our intelligence, our gifts, our energy, our skills, our stocks, our dog, our strut, our job, and our life. The reality of stewardship is harsh: We can possess nothing but our name and a claim on God's grace. When fully first realized, the concept of stewardship can take the wind out of the most inflated sails.

The news gets better. With humility comes an even greater realization: God calls each one of us to our job, to do his work. To take care of his creation. To manage his resources as he would. We possess his power of attorney for management decision making. When someone requests references, we can drop the name of the Creator and Sustainer of the cosmos. When money is an issue, we can sharpen our pencils in the light of eternity.

More than correct theology, stewardship is a powerful philosophy that permeates all of life and work. "Stewardship is not a subcategory of the

Christian life," wrote Randy Alcorn in *Money, Possessions and Eternity*. "Stewardship is the Christian life."[4] Stewardship is first an internal reality, affecting the way a person thinks, sees, and feels. Stewardship anchors motivation. Once inside our heart and mind, stewardship eventually and inevitably works its way out.

> Stewardship is first an internal reality, affecting the way a person thinks, sees, and feels. Stewardship anchors motivation. Once inside our heart and mind, stewardship eventually and inevitably works its way out.

As with the widow who tossed her last two coins into the temple treasury, stewardship evidences how much of ourselves we've invested in the work we return unto God. Likewise, consider a friend of ours as a modern-day steward with his Christmas bonus. For years, he has taken his bonus to the bank and cashed the ten-thousand-dollar-plus check for a fistful of hundred-dollar bills. He then distributes the money anonymously into mailboxes of families he knows are in need. He has come to grips with the fact that his possessions are not really his.

For Bold Assurance Ministries, founded by Bert Decker, stewardship shows up as repositioned intellectual capital. Oral communication training programs originally sold through Decker Communications became the foundational principles and techniques in the Bold Assurance programs used to teach people how to share their faith effectively with others.

In day-to-day living, stewardship knows no limits. There is no blank in which we check off "done."

The Mind of Service: A Body of Work

On certain days, you might just catch Bill Pollard, the CEO at ServiceMaster, wearing a pair of overalls, sweeping the hallways. While it is only a symbolic gesture—a way to drive home the point at the company's annual "We Serve Day"—you would be mistaken to believe that Pollard was in disguise. Like the name of the company he manages, he is both a servant and a master: a leader whose primary task is to serve. At ServiceMaster, the "assets" are not so much the services they provide—lawn care, pest control, housekeeping, food service, and plant operations—but their people. Each person, created in the image of God, represents a living storehouse of creative potential. In its purpose statement, ServiceMaster lists four interconnected objectives:

- To honor God in all that we do.
- To help people develop.
- To pursue excellence.
- To grow profitably.

The methodology makes the objectives apparent. The management and staff work to develop the potential of each person—not as a unit of economic production, but fully across the range of human qualities: physically, emotionally, intellectually, and spiritually. To do so requires a grand inversion of sorts: the people traditionally considered "entry-level" workers—janitors or rookie salespeople, for example—are encouraged to take initiative while those in the higher echelons adopt the role of servants. By caring for and nurturing employees "under them," managers are expected to turn a person accustomed to being an "object" of work into a "subject" of work; that is, to make work a vital part of who a person is instead of just something he or she does.

Wise stewardship, driven by a servant's heart, is the core reality of ServiceMaster. Although founded by followers of Christ and built on biblical principles, ServiceMaster practices inclusion: the company hires people regardless of religious beliefs. The mandate is this: made in the image of God, every person deserves to be treated with respect, care, and dignity. Throughout the hierarchy of the company, weaving together the various structural levels, is a single question: *At the end of the day, are the resources and assets I have been given to manage better or worse?* Even though "resources and assets" include all elements of a person's job—financial accounts, office space, maintenance, and customer service—the overriding focus is developing the company's greatest asset: its people. Managers must continually evaluate themselves with this perspective: *Through their work, are our employees closer to being the kind of people God created them to be?*

How do managers know that stewardship of their people asset is a priority? The marble statue in front of the Chicago headquarters depicts Christ washing the feet of an apostle. Just beyond the statue is a wall where employees with at least twenty-five years of service to the company have their names chiseled in granite. For ServiceMaster, the pulse of stewardship is nothing less than a servant's heart.

For Bill Pollard, Bert Decker, our friend with the fistful of hundred-dollar bills each Christmas, and countless others, work has become a matter of responsibility exercised in an environment of trust and care.

Stewardship: Our Accountability

Ancient literature often pictures the steward as the manager of a large estate. The job of the steward literally was to stand in for the owner during sustained absence, such as business travel or military duty. During that time, the steward was responsible to protect and grow the value of everything within the boundaries of the estate. Upon return, the owner had expectations of not only maintenance, but improvement. He trusted in the steward's productive work.

A steward's work is to serve the purposes of the owner. A body of work, if it is to obtain real and lasting value, must spring from the mind of a servant. A "trustee" is a modern-day synonym for the work of a steward. A trustee, by definition, is "entrusted" with the responsibility of supervision, management, and growth. Webster's definition of "entrust" is an equally powerful description of the covenant between God and his workers: "to commit with confidence."

> Stewardship does not stop—or even start—with giving God a 10-percent stake in our bucks. A more accurate picture, in fact, would look like this: God has totally funded our working life's bank account with 100 percent of the venture capital.

Stewardship does not stop—or even start—with giving God a 10-percent stake in our bucks. A more accurate picture, in fact, would look like this: God has totally funded our working life's bank account with 100 percent of the venture capital.

God does not blindly yield his assets to be squandered freely or made to serve purposes other than his own. Contrary to much public opinion, he is not a dawdler or a kindly and senile benefactor, but the God of the cosmos who eventually will hold people accountable for the quality of their work.

Paul issued this warning:

By the grace God has given me, I laid a foundation as an expert builder, and someone else is building on it. But each one should be careful how he builds. For no one can lay any foundation other than the one already laid, which is Jesus Christ. If any man builds on this foundation using gold, silver, costly stones, wood, hay or straw, his work will be shown for what it is, because the Day will bring it to light. It will be revealed with fire, and the fire will test the quality of each man's work. If what he has built survives, he will receive his reward. If it is burned up, he will suffer loss; he himself will be saved, but only as one escaping through the flames. (1 Cor. 3:10–15)

Our work matters to God. It cannot save us, but it is of value. As stewards, ones entrusted with assets, we are responsible for what we do and more important, how we do it. We are to serve God's purposes, giving him glory and serving others. In our work, we should have the heart and mind of the great Servant:

Do nothing out of selfish ambition or vain conceit, but in humility consider others better than yourselves. Each of you should look not only to your own interests, but also to the interests of others.

Your attitude should be the same as that of Christ Jesus,

Who, being in very nature God,
did not consider equality with God
something to be grasped,
but made himself nothing,
taking the very nature of a servant,
being made in human likeness. (Phil. 2:3–7)

We are accountable for the quality of our work. Periodically on the job, we expect overt, structured, formal evaluations: customer-satisfaction surveys, peer critiques, project reviews, skill assessments, product-knowledge tests, and performance appraisals with our supervisors. In our professional roles, these evaluations can provide invaluable feedback to us.

The primary tools of evaluation from God about our work are introspective; overall we must ask ourselves: *Did we serve the purposes of God and the benefit of others?* Specifically, we must identify all the assets and resources God has put in our care:

- What are my gifts, and how am I using them as God intended?
- Are my relationships honoring God? Am I helping to develop and lead others to God?
- How am I managing my time? Am I putting every twenty-four hours to the best use?
- Am I using my network of connections for God's work?
- Is my influence counting for the kingdom?
- Have I won awards and recognition that would bring honor to God as my Creator?
- How did I do with last year's opportunities?
- How am I positioned to face next year's challenges?
- Am I on target with my life mission?

We must always listen for the voice of God, a still, small whisper heard far away from the "busy-ness" of business.

Retired General Colin Powell should know a thing or two about the accountability of stewardship. During the Desert Shield and Desert Storm operations in the early nineties, he became accountable to the American public almost daily with his military briefings. Whether on the battlefield or currently on a basketball court with a group of inner-city kids under the auspices of his America's Promise campaign for volunteers among corporate America, General Powell concludes:

> Selfishness is innate; each of us is born selfish. Stewardship—caring about others, sacrificing for others—is something we learn as we grow up. My extended family taught me my first lessons in stewardship. . . .
>
> As a career solider, I naturally felt a primary responsibility for keeping America safe. Every man or woman in uniform knows that he or she may one day be called upon to make the ultimate sacrifice for our country. That is certainly stewardship of the highest order. Short of that, I am reminded of a saying we have in the Army: "Officers eat last." Taking care of your soldiers is also an act of stewardship.[5]

And finally General Powell brings stewardship down to the individual person and family:

> Families who do good works together usually find their life as a family is strengthened and enriched. . . . If we don't do our part as good citizens— if we are not good stewards—we will soon find that our individual quality of life is diminished along with the quality of community life. So the two [parenting and community] are really different sides of the same coin.[6]

Clearly, stewardship empowered through service as a goal differs drastically from the goals set by most American businesses. But capitalism shares this with our work as followers of Jesus: a fierce intensity to protect and grow whatever assets are under our control. Stewardship is a deep, burning passion to involve heart, mind, body, and soul to powerfully manage all of who we are and what he has given us for the advancement of his kingdom. Work should involve 100 percent of each one of us. We are in constant competition to do better with what we've been entrusted. We should share the intensity of the fiercest CEO: to maximize return on investment.

> Work should involve 100 percent of each one of us. We are in constant competition to do better with what we've been entrusted. We should share the intensity of the fiercest CEO: to maximize return on investment.

In the parable of the talents, Jesus told a story to illustrate the necessity of a passion and diligence to multiply what we have been entrusted:

> It will be like a man going on a journey, who called his servants and entrusted his property to them. To one he gave five talents of money, to another two talents, and to another one talent, each according to his ability. Then he went on his journey. The man who had received the five talents went at once and put his money to work and gained five more. So also, the one with the two talents gained two more. But the man who had received the one talent went off, dug a hole in the ground and hid his master's money.
>
> After a long time the master of those servants returned and settled

accounts with them. The man who had received the five talents brought the other five. "Master," he said, "you entrusted me with five talents. See, I have gained five more."

His master replied, "Well done, good and faithful servant! You have been faithful with a few things; I will put you in charge of many things. Come and share your master's happiness!"

The man with the two talents also came. "Master," he said, "you entrusted me with two talents; see, I have gained two more."

His master replied, "Well done, good and faithful servant! You have been faithful with a few things; I will put you in charge of many things. Come and share your master's happiness!"

Then the man who had received the one talent came. "Master," he said, "I knew that you are a hard man, harvesting where you have not sown and gathering where you have not scattered seed. So I was afraid and went out and hid your talent in the ground. See, here is what belongs to you."

His master replied, "You wicked, lazy servant! So you knew that I harvest where I have not sown and gather where I have not scattered seed? Well then, you should have put my money on deposit with the bankers, so that when I returned I would have received it back with interest.

"Take the talent from him and give it to the one who has the ten talents. For everyone who has will be given more, and he will have an abundance. Whoever does not have, even what he has will be taken from him. And throw that worthless servant outside, into the darkness, where there will be weeping and gnashing of teeth." (Matt. 25:14–30)

Some would say a business founded on stewardship would get eaten alive in the jaws of corporate cannibals. Not so. To put it bluntly: Stewardship is good business.

That's not, however, why Bill Amick, chairman and CEO of Amick Farms in Batesburg, South Carolina, has committed his business to God. Because he sees himself as steward rather than owner, he offers employees competitive wages and benefits. He also started a company chaplaincy program in 1992 to meet the spiritual needs of more than 1,200 workers of different ethnic backgrounds. Today, Amick Farms has one part-time and two full-time chaplains.

> To put it bluntly: Stewardship is good business.

Bill Amick's company consistently ranks atop his industry by a benchmarking service that compares cost and marketing efficiencies. While not the largest poultry company in production volume, its numbers are impressive: two hundred thousand chicks hatched daily, six days a week; 750,000 chickens processed each week. Annual sales consistently top $100 million.

Care breeds passion. Maturity yields discernment. Dignity drives energy. Polished skills smooth tensions. Talents produce profit.

ServiceMaster is another prime example. Make no mistake about it: ServiceMaster is no weak-kneed sister in the world of competitive business. Based in Downers Grove, Illinois, and founded in 1929, the company presently employs fifty-thousand people, manages another two hundred thousand, operates in thirty-eight countries, and has more than 6.5 million customers. Its businesses run the gamut from Terminix Pest Control, TruGreen-Chemlawn, and Merry Maids to plant operations and maintenance for nursing homes and schools. In 1999, the company generated more than $5.7 billion in revenues. The company has grown for the past twenty-eight consecutive years, with total profit growth over the last three-, ten-, and twenty-year periods exceeding 20 percent, which is substantially higher than market averages.

Winning more than its share of prestigious awards and accolades, including the Horatio Alger Award, ServiceMaster has been universally praised for its vitality and studied aggressiveness. Many experts have listed it as a top three- to five-year stock pick.

To paraphrase the master in the parable of the talents: *That's all well and good, as it should be.*

CAUGHT IN THE PEDAL-TO-THE-METAL PACE:
FINDING REST

HEINRICH BARTH, AN *explorer of the Sahara Desert, was a restless man; in all of his journeys, he never found what he was looking for: life-giving relationships with other human beings. His soul was as vast and dry and barren as the terrain he traveled.*

Born in Germany, the son of a prosperous, self-made merchant, Barth, even in his childhood, was never content with standing still. For the love of his mother, he became obsessed with becoming more successful than his father. As a child, he studied tenaciously and excelled in archaeology, geography, language, and history, which appear to be an eclectic mix except for this fact: at the core, his studies were about other places and other times. All of his life, Barth seemed a stranger who was always in motion. A brilliant loner, Barth compiled vocabularies of more than forty native dialects, but could never find a way to truly connect with others.

The Sahara, a desert larger than the United States, fascinated Barth. Two nearly simultaneous disappointments launched him into an exploration of the Sahara: his failure as a geography teacher (he possessed a chronic inability to relate to others) and an abrupt breakup with the woman he had been intensely courting. In the same batch of mail that contained his sweetheart's letter of rejection was an invitation to join an expedition into the African interior.

In March of 1850, at the age of twenty-eight, Heinrich Barth departed from Tripoli to explore the Sahara Desert. Six years and ten thousand miles later, his expedition was over. Along the way, Barth witnessed the deaths of the expedition leader and a good friend, both of malaria. He found striking evidence of a Roman settlement along a dry river valley, and a series of rock paintings depicting elephants and ostriches. The Sahara, he discovered, was not always a desert but, like Barth, was in constant motion, restless, swirling.

He had made detailed maps and drawings and learned integral facts about the civilizations of the desert. To survive among often-hostile conditions and cultures, he had carried a Colt six-shooter, assumed the pose of a holy man, and once— trapped overnight in a barren, sun-baked mountain cave—sucked his own blood to cure his thirst. Long since separated from the original expedition, he was gone so long that, back in Europe, he eventually was presumed dead.

Although Barth laid the groundwork for future trade agreements and vital routes of essential commerce, he never accomplished what he really wanted. In August of 1855, he returned home, exhausted. Even as he was being honored as one of the great explorers of his time (he earned the prestigious Patron's Medal of the Royal Geographic Society), he retreated into himself: a recluse, an explorer who could never quite discover himself or the secret to relationship. For the next three years, he wrote a five-volume publication about his journey that was judged to be "credible, but dull." In 1863, at the age of forty-two, he returned to the University of Berlin as a geography teacher. Two years later, he died of a stomach ailment developed during his long travels.

The pain may have felt a little like an unresolved hunger. A deep restlessness.

A Restless Society

We live in a restless age. An age of hearts filled with bristling static. Of unbridled lust and greed, the inevitable violence of unanchored souls. Of superficial technological connections—cell phones, web pages, fax machines, pagers, chat rooms, and satellite beams. Of entangling and comforting noise, our backgrounds filled with drumbeats and electronic beeps and turbine screams. Of spoken, straightforward demands—calm and flat and insistent—to perform.

Every year, every month, every week, every day, every moment is filled with *something* that not only *has* to be done but has to be done by *us*. A 1998 Reuters report claims that the average worker today gets interrupted 169 times each day.[1] These interruptions keep us in a high state of torque. The instinctive answer to the question "How are you?" is no longer "I'm fine." Instead it's: "Busy."

In his book *Sabbath*, Wayne Muller wrote:

> We say this to one another with no small degree of pride, as if our exhaustion were a trophy, our ability to withstand stress a mark of real

character. The busier we are, the more important we seem to ourselves and, we imagine, to others. To be unavailable to our friends and family, to be unable to find time for the sunset (or even to know that the sun has set at all), to whiz through our obligations without time for a single mindful breath, this has become the model of a successful life.[2]

Even our recreation is filled with engines of cacophony. Cutthroat softball. Power skating. Dual twin horses. Downhill racing. Freefall rides. Sanctioned biking. Ultralight camping. The goal to do it right, to do it best, to do it with more than a dash of panache. Adrenaline is important, the high watermark, the arrival point. Celerity equals celebrity. Exhaustion is a trophy. Rest, if it comes at all, is in the fact that you did it right. You gave it your best. Even badminton, these days, can get ruthless.

Increasingly, our play has become work.

Increasingly, our play has become work.

The lines between the two blur. A small-business owner recently spoke up in the middle of a Bible study session on marriage, "My wife says I shouldn't bring home work from the office. Like on Sunday afternoon, I get on the computer and do stuff. She thinks I'm working, but I love what I do. It's fun. But that's causing problems between us. I mean, is it working if I love it? Just tell me, is that work or play?"

We are confused.

Rest Rankles Us as Nonproductive

Walk into a mall on a Sunday—any mall, any Sunday. Take mental notes on what you see: movement. Registers beeping. Slashed prices. Eyes searching, calculating, measuring. Monies exchanged. Commerce flowing. Babies jostled, crying, tugging. Music carefully accelerated, in rhythm with the humming nature of acquisition. Restless teenagers prancing, bouncing, nervous, unsettled with hormones, desperate for the sweet drug of likability. Everywhere: the perpetual and strained motions of living, belonging. The order is in the chaos. The jangled, misdirected movements toward some sense of purpose or, failing that, possession.

It is hardly a place to practice the Sabbath—or so one would think. But you just might be wrong. In the food courts of the typical mall, with their endless chains of smells and people and coins, there is an odd and unset-

> Ours is an age that lacks nothing, except this: transcendent silence.

tling sense of displacement: like a swimmer wearing a parachute on a soccer field. One store is closed. The lights are off. You notice the gray stillness; it hisses a disturbing silence. No one is home. The first conclusion: the store is out of business, has to be, no other explanation possibly could exist. Sunday produces prime-time consumerism: a new religion feeding a great hunger. Why would a store—especially a food store—*not* be open?

Slightly mystified, you begin to look at the signs.

First: *Chick-fil-A.*

Then, lower: *Closed Sundays.*

On the drive home you have a few fleeting thoughts: *Did I pay too much for the Nikes?* And: *What's the deal with Chick-fil-A?*

Ours is an age that lacks nothing except this: transcendent silence. Something to take us beyond the noise, the temporal human stirrings of the world. Disconnected from divine purpose, we are afraid of ourselves. How little we might actually turn out to be. We cling to superficial static, which sounds like the racing of the heart.

Busy is better. Or is it?

Rest Is Part of the Productivity Rhythm

Even in our superheaded economy where business possibilities abound, rest has become suddenly fashionable. "Sleep, that rare commodity in stressed-out America, is the new status symbol," *Wall Street Journal* reporter Nancy Jeffrey wrote in 1999. "Once derided as a wimpish failing—the same 1980s overachievers who cried 'Lunch is for Losers' also believed 'Sleep is for Suckers'—slumber is now being touted as the restorative companion to the creative executive mind."[3]

Netscape cofounder Marc Andreesen, Amazon.com CEO Jeff Bezos, and Snapple creator Michael Weinstein are among the leading chief executives who, according to reporter Jeffrey, make a habit of getting at least eight hours of sleep each night.[4]

In God's creation, rest is the soft foil, the necessary pause. The time and place, if you will, to recognize the rhythm, to measure the divine heartbeat of the cosmos. For each day, there is night. For each summer, there is winter. For each spring, there is fall. For each birth, there is a death. In the poetry of Ecclesiastes:

> There is a time for everything,
>   and a season for every activity under heaven:
>
> a time to be born and a time to die,
> a time to plant and a time to uproot,
> a time to kill and a time to heal,
> a time to tear down and a time to build,
> a time to weep and a time to laugh,
> a time to weep and a time to dance,
> a time to scatter stones and a time to gather them,
> a time to embrace and a time to refrain,
> a time to search and a time to give up,
> a time to keep and a time to throw away,
> a time to tear and a time to mend,
> a time to be silent and a time to speak,
> a time to love and a time to hate,
> a time for war and a time for peace. (Eccl. 3:1–8)

Rest itself is an essential movement of the rhythm of life. "By the seventh day God had finished the work he had been doing; so on the seventh day he rested from all his work. And God blessed the seventh day and made it holy, because on it he rested from all the work of creating that he had done" (Gen. 2:2–3). All creation exercises rest, like a wave of music breathes sweet draughts of silence. In the rhythm of life, rest is necessary, inbred, integral, essential, intrinsic.

When your body and mind stay set on overdrive, they rebel: headaches. Muscle soreness. Stomach upset. Digestive problems. Hypertension. High blood pressure. Strokes. Heart attacks. Irritability. Sluggishness of thought. Lack of concentration. Weariness of spirit. Anxiety. Self-pity. Doubt. The desire to quit. Depression.

Without rest, the coiled springs of eternity unwind in temporal, mean-ingless, clanging motion of disconnected activity. Rest is the soul of work, the stillness at the center of a storm. Rest reminds us of our place and our purpose.

Immediately following the eloquent verses of Ecclesiastes is this curious reminder: "What does the worker gain from his toil? I have seen the burden God has laid on men. He has made everything beautiful in its time. He has also set eternity in the hearts of men; yet they can-not fathom what God has done from beginning to end" (Eccl. 3:9–11).

> **Rest reminds us of our place and our purpose.**

Rest temporarily and consistently reminds us that eternity resides in each heart—a place to fathom the works of God. Rest offers a pausing from work to reflect on God, to cultivate a balanced life, and to allow Jesus to help us accomplish our work.

The word *Sabbath* was formed from the Hebrew *shabath* and the Arabic *sabata*, meaning to cease, desist, or to intercept, interrupt. The language carries an intensive force, implying a willed and complete cessation—a *making* to cease. So necessary is this Sabbath that it carries overtones of implied violence: cease or else. It is like a kinder, gentler Clint Eastwood who begs you, with a smile, to make his day. At the same time, you instinctively know he's dead serious.

Holy days of doing nothing.

By contrast, commerce comes about through motion; it is a stream. To stop a stream—to forcibly cause its cessation—is to dam it. Some of commerce's central verbs—acquire, expand, control, manage, and leverage—get punchy with perceived insults. Business depends on *busy-ness*, perpetual outward movement. To stop is deadly. Is it any wonder that the business world has such a difficult time with the idea of a Sabbath?

To open his book *The Sabbath*, Abraham Joshua Heschel wrote:

> Technical civilization is man's conquest of space. It is a triumph fre-quently achieved by sacrificing an essential ingredient of existence, namely, time. In technical civilization, we expend time to gain space. To enhance our power in the world of space is our main objective. Yet to have more does not mean to be more. The power we attain in the world

of space terminates abruptly at the borderline of time. But time is the heart of existence.

To gain control over the world of space is certainly one of our tasks. The danger begins when in gaining power in the realm of space we forfeit all aspirations in the realm of time. There is a realm of time where the goal is not to have but to be, not to own but to give, not to control but to share, not to subdue but to be in accord. Life goes wrong when the control of space, the acquisition of things of space, becomes our sole concern.

Nothing is more useful than power, nothing more frightful. We have often suffered from degradation by poverty, now we are threatened with degradation through power. There is happiness in the love of labor, there is misery in the love of gain. Many hearts and pitchers are broken at the fountain of profit. Selling himself into a slavery of things, man becomes a utensil that is broken at the fountain.[5]

Space used to mean something to us. It reminded us of the rhythm of life. Night, unspoiled by the humming of electricity, more powerfully followed day. Sleep happened naturally; there was nothing else to do. Summer and winter, without the Dave Lennox heat pump, were bookends of extremes, sometimes survival. Spring and fall marked rebirth and death, not Scott's lawn care and Green Bay Packers pennants. Mortality was not hidden with Estee Lauder; it was the end of a powerful human cycle begun with birth. In such naked space, we could mark the passing of days, seasons, and lives. They formed a rhythm that sounded like the heart's eternal music. Our work mandated rest.

As Wayne Muller points out in *Sabbath*, we have lost this essential rhythm:

> Our culture invariably supposes that action and accomplishment are better than rest, that doing something—anything—is better than doing nothing. . . . Because of our desire to succeed, to meet those ever-growing expectations, we do not rest. Because we do not rest, we lose our way. We miss the compass points that would show us where to go, we bypass the nourishment that would give us succor. We miss the quiet that would give us wisdom. We miss the joy and love born of effortless delight. Poisoned by this hypnotic belief that good things come only through

unceasing determination and tireless effort, we can never truly rest. And for want of rest, our lives are in danger.[6]

With our technical successes, we have forgotten that control is an illusion. That space does not belong to us. That ownership is a lie. That possession is ungodly. That time, unspent, is vital. That rest empowers the world.

But evidently, few believe it. A recent British study showed that when people work sixty hours a week, their productivity decreases by 25 percent.[7]

Rest empowers the world.

Would it not seem more logical to work forty-five hours a week at 100 percent productivity? Is this typical extended-hours schedule yet another illustration of the law of diminishing returns?

In the Old Testament, the concept of the Sabbath did not simply apply to people. The land itself also required rest. God established elaborate rules and guidelines for the care—and rest—of the land. He mandated that Israel rotate crops to avoid stressing the soil. He commanded that every forty-ninth year, all of the land was to remain unplanted to give it a vital and complete rest.

Rest allows for a deep rooting in God; for crops, and much more so for people.

The rested soul is unstressed, ripe for seed. Potentially productive.

Rest Works as Reflection

Moses spent forty years on the backside of a hill with a herd of sheep before he undertook the assignment God gave him: plenty of time for creating character and sharpening stamina.

Saint Augustine talked of both active and contemplative life. While both play vital roles, the contemplative life of reflection, meditation, and prayer, he considered of greater value.

Truett and Dan Cathy, father and son, are deeply acquainted with both the contemplative and the active. For starters, they focused on fierce, tenacious, heart-reeling, mind-bending, gut-wrenching work. In 1946, a year after the end of World War II, Truett sold his car, combined savings with his younger brother, Ben, and borrowed some money to buy a tiny, twenty-four-hour restaurant in an Atlanta suburb. For $10,600, they bought the

Dwarf Grill—ten counter stools and four tables—and a gigantic dream. Work was a deeply woven family tradition, a liturgy of sorts.

When the children were toddlers, Truett's wife, Jeanette, would dress them up as dwarfs. They memorized jingles, and with the energy of rabbits in spring, they would bounce around, singing to the customers. When they were old enough to reach the counters, they could ring the register or wash the dishes. Above all, the Cathys wanted to share the disciplined joy of work, to spread it like leaves on the family tree. Truett Cathy brought up his children to work—and to work hard. God, he told his children, rejoices in our successes, not our failures.

If that is true, then God has been rejoicing a good deal over the Cathys during the last three decades. By the late sixties, Truett had developed what would be the staple of his business—the boneless chicken sandwich. At the time, there was nothing like it on the market. In 1967, he scored another coup—the pioneering of the in-mall fast-food restaurant with the opening of the first Chick-fil-A in Atlanta's Greenbriar Mall. The rest is history. Today, Chick-fil-A is the third-largest quick-service chicken restaurant company in the nation with more than 850 restaurants in thirty-five states and South Africa. In 1990, the company reached $300 million in annual sales, and *Business Atlanta* magazine named Truett Atlanta's Most Respected CEO.

The successes, however, derive from something more powerful than even hard work. Unlike many successful business people, Truett never succumbed to myopia, narrow obsession, or megalomania. He insists that no matter how large Chick-fil-A becomes, it is—measured against the overall scheme of things—a lesson in humility. He maintains a great responsibility to God for the way he conducts his life, of which his business is only a part.

The Moo-Cow Band has wedged its way into the thick of things. If the Moo-Cow Band conjures up a ragtag bunch of old geezers who don't have anything else in life going for them on a Saturday night, you're wrong. Truett's son Dan Cathy, an accomplished trumpeter, has put together a group of the best musical performers in Atlanta. They have played at the Peach Bowl, at political inaugurations, in churches all around the country. The Moo-Cow Band represents rest from the restaurant business.

Rest runs through all of life. Rest rounds out life. Rest funds life.

In addition to making a profit, Chick-fil-A has served the greater good.

Truett's family has remained deeply connected—to each other, to God, and to the need in the world around them. Chick-fil-A has established generous scholarship programs for company employees. The WinShape Centre, a foster care program and camp, raises funds for children who are "victims of circumstances." Service, not blind profit, is the overriding agenda at Chick-fil-A. And while that agenda has cost the company some dollars, it has been rewarding beyond the Cathys' wildest dreams.

So how, in a culture obsessed with getting ahead, have the Cathys been able to maintain a perspective that includes seeing the needs around them? More than anything else, it has to do with those unlit stores on Sunday. When all the world is spinning in commerce around them, the Cathys are resting. On Sundays, all of the Chick-fil-A restaurants are closed.

Does the Sunday closing cost them profits? You figure it out. According to the National Restaurant Association, Sunday historically is the third-most active day for restaurant sales, trailing only Friday and Saturday and generating 14.2 percent of the week's business. Of the roughly $50 billion spent in restaurants on Sundays each year, none of it will be spent at Chick-fil-A.[8] The Cathys don't condemn others who open on Sundays; in fact, they eat out from time to time on Sunday. But closing their own restaurant on Sunday is their personal way of honoring the Lord's Day.

But the question persists: Do the Cathys' work ethic and their rest ethic make good business sense? Truett believes it to be one of the best business decisions their company has ever made. The policy of rest each week helps attract and retain good employees, both in management and on the front line. Chick-fil-A has one of the lowest turnover rates in the industry. "We feel we make up the difference. We feel we have been blessed by closing on Sunday. For the most part, we generate the sales in six days that our competitors do in seven days."

Although they can point to the bottom line as empirical proof, their inner measuring stick has different markings. Sabbath is more than Sunday closing. For the Cathys, the Sabbath is more than just a disciplined tradition of rest and relaxation. It is, they say, the very lifeblood of their faith, their souls, and their business.

We often feel jerked back and forth between business commitments, church activities, and family responsibilities. While busy responding to the needs of a child or a spouse, we feel guilty about letting our boss, colleagues, or customers down at work. While working to meet the demands of our job, we feel guilty about not being at church. While at church, we feel guilty about missing a celebration with our child.

Without the rhythm of rest, the jerking continually grows more violent. We like Wayne Muller's analogy in *Sabbath*:

> Without rest, we respond from a survival mode, where everything we meet assumes a terrifying prominence. When we are driving a motorcycle at high speed, even a small stone in the road can be a deadly threat. So, when we are moving faster and faster, every encounter, every detail inflates in importance, everything seems more urgent than it really is, and we react with sloppy desperation.[9]

Others notice when we ourselves don't experience rest. Imagine yourself lining up five people who work with or for you to characterize your life at work. Would you hear something like this: "He's obsessed. It looks like he's constantly on a treadmill. Expand, expand, expand. He's trying to control everything, but things are still falling between the cracks. Too many deadlines. Too many projects. Never says no. He hasn't taken a vacation in three years. He's simply driven."

The picture of this frantic life reminds us of a breaker box. You load up a circuit and everything runs fine until there's one surge of energy above the threshold. *Bam*—everything goes black. Rest allows the light to stay on without our pushing ourselves beyond the threshold where everything goes black for us. Too many of us run too close to the threshold. Depression is simply the depletion of emotional energy.

Still, rest is not a capacity issue. Many of us have the capacity to work hard. We jump out of bed in high gear, work nonstop all day, go to bed, and then tomorrow do the same thing, year in and year out. And if you're a salesperson getting paid to work ten to twelve hours a day, then that's how you need to work. As business owners ourselves, we'd tell you, "Don't bring your need for a Sabbath to the office on Monday morning. We pay you for work. Rest and reflect on your own time."

But do rest. Rest represents your personal recouping activities or nonactivities. Others at work will notice whether you've rested by your input, productivity, and attitude when you show up week after week.

David wrote of the rest God promised:

> The LORD is my Shepherd,
> I shall not be in want.
> He makes me lie down in green pastures,
> he leads me beside quiet waters,
> he restores my soul. (Ps. 23:1–3)

This is the picture of physical, mental, and spiritual rest. Claim it as God's promise, and consider it your personal responsibility, pursuit, and privilege.

Rest Reminds Us of God's Holiness

Following six days of creation, God created the seventh day and "made it holy" (Gen. 2:3)—set apart from the everyday. This is the first reference to holiness in the Bible. The Sabbath represents a sacred moment in time to contemplate eternity. Wrote Heschel:

> The higher goal of spiritual living is not to amass a wealth of informa-
> tion. . . . Spiritual life begins to decay when we fail to see the grandeur of
> what is eternal in time. . . .
>   Time and space are interrelated. To overlook either of them is to be
> partially blind. What we plead against is man's unconditional surrender
> to space, his enslavement to things. We must not forget that it is not a
> thing that lends significance to a moment; it is a moment that lends sig-
> nificance to a thing.[10]

In the absence of a holy Sabbath, the world degenerates into a temporal, superficial, sensory, diminutive reality. As poet Wallace Stevens wrote:

> We keep coming back and coming back
> To the real: to the hotel instead of the hymns
> That fall upon it out of the wind.[11]

We are left without holy ground, a greater purpose to sanctify human existence. Hotels—and those who build them—eventually fall down and decay. *Vanity*, screams the teacher in Ecclesiastes, *all is vanity!* The world is insane. The Sabbath, practiced and believed, keeps us sane.

Dan Cathy knows this: The business world is designed to eat you alive. To consume you. At its core, business is concerned about expanding temporary realties: productivity, budgets, profits, lever-age, capital, and power. It revels in the concrete and the replication of the temporal. It is nour-ished on the idea that things—being things—

> The Sabbath, practiced and believed, keeps us sane.

must be renewed and replaced. It counts on the intrinsic brokenness of the world. There is very little eternal about it, except the driving and curious notion of legacy.

For a follower of Christ, the Fourth Frontier is an easy place to get lost. With its singular, temporal focus on spatial reality, the business world is lit-tered with burnouts, megalomaniacs, high-tech neurotics, precise and stumbling drunkards of power, and people who seldom look at the stars.

This is a given: the follower of Christ will experience great stress, in the binding—often paralyzing—friction between spatial and eternal realities. Friction heats things up, accelerates motion, tempts you to get swept along. Dan Cathy says that no formula exists to deal with the inevitable stress. As we stated in an earlier chapter, the true integrator of faith and business *cannot* rely on a fixed and graduated list of priorities:

1. God first.
2. Family second.
3. Church third.
4. Work fourth (and, of course, last).

Faith is not meant to clunk along like a blocky, broken-down Edsel. Life bathed in faith is a matter of sacrifice, a process of discerning what is next on the to-do list of life. Sometimes the family must make sacrifices. Sometimes, the church will have to make do without the Cathys for a while. And some-times the business, forever champing at the bit, must be bridled in.

Dan Cathy remembers when he once had to make a choice between lunch with the chairman of Coca-Cola and saying good-bye to his son at the air-port. He chose his son. Under different circumstances, he might have cho-sen the chairman. "There doesn't have to be an ironclad rule that a family has to come before business or that your church has to come before business," says Truett. "It's a matter of blending it altogether."

But working hard is very important. "People like to follow people who are excited about their work, but not workaholics." Truett Cathy puts people who work long hours into two categories: those who do it because they enjoy what they do ("It's not really work when you're doing the thing you enjoy," he says), and those who do it for some ulterior motive—money, pride, selfish ambition. People in the second group lack balance.

Spirituality is an ever-elusive search to engage true discernment. Sometimes there is a fine line between the leading of the Holy Spirit and a mild heartburn from Papa John's pizza.

For an explorer of the Fourth Frontier, the Sabbath is an oasis, a fount of water in the Sahara Desert. It refreshes and nourishes. It is vital and essential. It prevents work from sucking your lifeblood. For the Cathys, the Sabbath is not simply a defensive strategy—a way to prevent consumption—but an aggressive catalyst of stewardship. Consistently reminded of eternity, Dan Cathy is able to expand his focus beyond the corporate horizon, to see with the eyes of heaven. From there he reclaims the perspective of stewardship: the careful and productive management of God's resources. He understands the necessity for innovation and creativity, which spring from a rested mind rooted in the life and love of God.

> Sabbath provides perspective on true power: where it comes from and how it's to be used.

In the business of stewardship, a believer can get no further than the vitality of his or her own life. Jesus said, "Remain in me, and I will remain in you. No branch can bear fruit by itself; it must remain in the vine. Neither can you bear fruit unless you remain in me" (John 15:4). Sabbath provides perspective on true power: where it comes from and how it's to be used.

Sabbath Is Serious Business

The Sabbath, of course, is not an unfamiliar idea to the business arena. But it has gained new attention, like other work/family issues. Most frequently, the sabbatical has been part of the academic life. After teaching for several semesters, professors take a paid leave to go away and refresh themselves, reflect on their learning, and return rested. But historically, because professors have been so underpaid, they have used the time away to write, publish, and teach in a different setting to make up the salary shortfall. Consequently, they often return to their full-time teaching assignment more tired than when they left.

But more and more organizations in the business sector have begun to reexamine the idea of the sabbatical. In a tight labor market, the sabbatical leave may make the difference in hiring and retaining the best minds.

Our church provides a great example. Every seven years, a pastoral minister receives a month's sabbatical with only two stipulations:First, the minister agrees to spend some time in personal reflection. Second, the minister must investigate some topic of interest related to his or her ministry. There is no dissertation to write, no sermon to create, no report to give to the elders. Just exploration and reflection.

Another case in point: our vacation that turned into our future. Ever since we began our business life together, we have taken our wives with us to enjoy a seven- to ten-day vacation. Part of our agenda on these shared vacations is to reflect on the bigger picture and purpose of our lives: are we still moving in the direction we need to move? Does God still have his hand on our lives and our business? Have we experienced any failures or setbacks that should cause us to question our methods? How do we feel about our Cornerstone Group friendship? How does our integrity measure up? Do we need to redirect any efforts? If so, which, why, how, where, and when?

The Life@Work Company was born on the beaches of the Cayman Islands in a conversation with our wives about the fact that some of the pieces of our mission statement (blending biblical wisdom and business excellence through consulting, teaching, mentoring, and writing) had not yet materialized. Actually, Tom was talking; Steve was complaining: "We're never going to realize that mission statement unless we do something radically and structurally different with our organization." That remark led us to reflect on how we'd begun together in the early days. We had scribbled out our mission statement on a napkin during breakfast at a local restaurant. We continued to have breakfast together for weeks and weeks because our whole agenda back then was to clearly articulate where we wanted to go: a road map for a lifetime of work together. We selected consulting because no one would ever pay us a nickel to hear us speak. So for years, we consulted in organizational change: helping the directional leader and his or her direct reports navigate their organization through strategic change. We brought in other consultants to help us with our business.

Our organization ripped along fine, we paid the bills, our wives were happy. The nagging concern, however, was still that we had not fully turned our total mission statement into reality. But our wives indulged us this one more effort: we added Sean Womack, a creative genius in marketing and brand development, as a partner to help us launch The Life@Work Company, and we began to think globally about the issue of integrating faith in the workplace.

All of that—the structure, the team, the risk, the capital, the passion, the energy—came as a result of our sabbatical on the beach in Cayman Islands.

For other people, reflective rest may mean not the birth of a new idea, but the death of an old one. Richard Graham (not his real name) became a consultant with one of the top three consulting firms during his early career. His career simply exploded, and he found himself gobbling up more and more responsibilities in a larger and larger territory. His titles changed almost faster than he could get his business cards reprinted, and the accompanying salary went through the roof. In the thick of things, he boarded a plane every Sunday night or Monday morning, not to return until Friday or Saturday night. But after he married and had a baby girl, he found himself wanting a different lifestyle that didn't fit the success model to which he'd grown accustomed. After a reflective, soul-searching sabbatical, he decided to have a conversation with his boss.

"What do you mean, you want to stop traveling?" his boss asked.

"Just call it a demotion. I'd like to transfer into another area that would not demand such a heavy workload and travel schedule."

His boss did not embrace his new idea. In fact, he trumped it. He offered him another promotion and salary jump that would have quickened even his then racing pulse.

So Richard demoted himself. Turning down the promotion and raise, he transferred to another job and soon left the company to join a different consulting practice more in line with his values. The courage to take that risk came from his sabbatical of reflection.

We all need to stretch the fabric of our lives to incorporate the concept of rest and reflection.

Not to Rest Is Sin

The Sabbath was pre-Fall: before all the bad stuff like violence and pimples and embezzlement and thorns and greed and the smell of Ben Gay. That's how rooted in the reality of the cosmos it is; not simply a stop-gap preventive, a Dutch Boy's finger in a big, terrible black hole. It is part of the rhythm of eternal, perfect, gorgeous life.

Imagine, then, its importance in a fallen world. With the ultimate *s-word*—sin. In today's world, of course, a great deal of confusion exists about the idea of sin. Sin is not some outdated, irrelevant idea of being naughty. It has not, contrary to published reports, been replaced by the more progressive notions of genetic determination, or a willy-nilly, namby-pamby grace of some unknown, unnamed divine pie in the sky. It is, theologically speaking, damned serious business.

Rest requires faith. It takes faith not to work on the Sabbath—faith not to worry about getting left behind, about getting everything done, about pressure from peers who don't observe a biblical rest.

From the perspective of the Sabbath, sin is cosmic stress. According to the *American Heritage* dictionary, stress is "an applied force or system of forces that tends to strain or deform a body." Theologically, sin is an incredibly dynamic force that distorts and warps. Sin prevents us from becoming fully human. It deforms us, reduces us to base desire. In sin's paralyzing fear and blindness, it is hard not to see ourselves pitted against others in perpetual motion.

Rest requires faith. It takes faith not to work on the Sabbath—faith not to worry about getting left behind, about getting everything done, about pressure from peers who don't observe a biblical rest. A life of faith is always tested in a context where people who don't live by faith seem to do better by violating the tenets of the faith.

Sometimes we pass the test. Such is the story that Chuck Colson tells in his classic autobiography, *Born Again*. During the time near his conversion to Jesus, Colson visited his longtime friend Tom Phillips, president of Raytheon Corporation. Colson wrote,

When I entered his office, it was the same old Tom, jet-black hair, athletic build, stripped down to the shirt-sleeves as always. But the smile was a lot warmer, radiant, in fact, and he looked more relaxed than I had ever seen him. In the old days, though always genial, he had a harried look—with phones ringing, secretaries running in and out of his office, his desk piled high with paper. Now there was something serene about his office as well as about Tom.[12]

The change in Phillips's surroundings and demeanor was dramatic: "There was a new compassion in his eyes and a gentleness in his voice," Colson continues. After about twenty minutes of conversation, Colson finally brought up what he had heard about Phillips's involvement in religious activity. "Yes, that's true, Chuck," his colleague replied. "I have accepted Jesus Christ. I have committed my life to Him and it has been the most marvelous experience of my whole life."[13]

> A lifestyle of biblical rest lived out in a harried world of work attracts attention.

Initially, Phillips's response shocked Colson. But the rest and peace the Raytheon executive demonstrated that day played a key role in Colson's conversion months later. A lifestyle of biblical rest lived out in a harried world of work attracts attention.

Business is stressful. Perhaps more than any human effort, commerce possesses the greatest potential to create cosmic turmoil, to pummel the paradoxical truth of eternity expressed by Jesus: "I tell you the truth, unless a kernel of wheat falls to the ground and dies, it remains only a single seed. But if it dies, it produces many seeds. The man who loves his life will lose it, while the man who hates his life in this world will keep it for eternal life" (John 12:24–25).

Life is about giving ourselves away, spreading seeds in eternity. Commerce demands acquisition, measurable growth, bottom-line proofs. Between the two perspectives, there's awful potential for great stress. The Sabbath is cosmic stress management.

A farmer, too, knows about stress. For any number of reasons, plants can become stressed: pests, disease, too much or too little sun or water, not enough nourishment. We are the fruit. Jesus is the vine. Sabbath represents a holy and rested soil.

Like many committed followers of Christ, Dan Cathy cannot exactly put into words specifically what the Sabbath requires. "It is not necessarily recreation, although that can be involved. It is not simply refreshment, although that will often be the result. It is not religious attention, but that often helps. It is not just relaxation, though tension often slips away."

Leaders in some contemporary churches have an equally difficult time describing the concept of rest and leading believers to practice it. From Friday evening until Sunday night, we simply accept other work "assignments": attend this conference. Meet with this committee. Visit this group. Study for your session. Plan this function. Practice this music. Organize this outreach. By the time we go back to Universal, Inc., on Monday morning, we're exhausted. The results: Christian workers often disappoint nonbelieving bosses and colleagues with their lack of productivity while recovering from the weekend of doing—church or otherwise. The contemporary organized church often falls short in helping believers observe the Sabbath along biblical lines.

In fact, when we seek to define our specific responsibilities in Sabbath, we miss the point. As business leaders, we are comfortable with agenda—a specific list of things to do with excellence, energy, and passion. We want to excel. That's probably why so many of us are so poorly acquainted with the idea of Sabbath.

Sabbath does not ask for our doing; in fact, it demands, by definition, the very cessation of our doing. The Sabbath does not represent legalism. It is not about a list of do's and don'ts on a certain day of the week. The Sabbath saturates us with a reason and time to *be* rather than do: to be a human be-ing. To recognize that, from the perspective of eternity, the work of creation already has been accomplished. That things, in the end, will turn out on the side of grace, truth, beauty, and love. We are, in a cosmic manner of speaking, simply along for the joyride. That is the message of the Sabbath.

Rest involves something we do, something we experience, something we demonstrate, and something God gives us. Rest and work do not represent contrasts; they are balanced parts of the same rhythm. You can't work well without rest, and you can't rest well without work.

If we don't work, we are lazy. We don't provide resources. We can't fulfill our calling. If we don't rest, we are shallow. We don't assess our direction.

We can't worship God. The Bible places both verbs, work and rest, side by side; both are good. Both actions require deliberate focus to succeed.

And when Monday morning rolls around again, we are reminded that God calls us to participate, in a specific time and place, in his eternal, accomplished work—rested and ready.

CREATIVE COLONIZATION:
EXPANDING YOUR INFLUENCE

JAMES COOK WAS *an unlikely choice to lead a scientific expedition for the British Navy in 1768. Although a veteran of the high seas, the thirty-nine-year-old lieutenant lacked the reputation of aristocratic heroes of the South Pacific such as Commodore John Byron and Captain Samuel Wallis.*

Cook had been in the Royal Navy for only ten years. Much of his training had come in the merchant marine. But while many Londoners had never heard of him, Cook had gained some acclaim within the Royal Geographic Society for his skills as an explorer and mapmaker. He had spent four years charting with great precision the various bays and inlets along the coast of Newfoundland, a work that proved invaluable to the British Navy in its battles against French strongholds in Canada. And the Admiralty considered his seamanship solid.

So Cook was given command of H. M. Bark Endeavour, *which, like him, was much more capable than a surface look suggested.* Endeavour, *before the Navy refashioned and renamed her, originally was a coal transport ship—the very type upon which Cook had trained as a teenager. Her size and shape made her perfect for carrying the equipment and personnel needed for the scientific expedition to Tahiti.*

Cook, his crew, and several scientists set sail on the Endeavour *with the expressed mission of observing the transit of Venus across the sun. The idea was that scientists could calculate the distance from the earth to the sun by timing this eclipse, which would occur in 1769 and not again until 1874. British scientists wanted to be in the perfect position to record and study the event. But the trip had a second goal, one that wasn't publicized: to search for what geographers believed was a southern continent that kept the world in balance.*

Cook never found such a continent, but he did become arguably the greatest explorer in Great Britain's history. In addition to his discoveries of vast land in the Pacific—much of which Great Britain colonized and some of which other European powers colonized—Cook was among the first seamen to take seriously the impact of diet and cleanliness on the health of sailors. In a time when ships routinely lost hundreds of sailors to scurvy, Cook maintained a remarkably low death rate because he required his men to wash daily and to eat fresh fruits, soups, and sauerkraut.

With mostly healthy crews, Cook made three multiyear expeditions that took him across a map of the world that, until he arrived, hadn't been drawn. While circling the globe twice, Cook became the first European to visit New Zealand, and in 1770 he claimed the eastern coast of Australia for Great Britain. On another voyage, Cook circled Antarctica, although it would be nearly seventy more years before anyone proved that it was a land continent and not just a mass of ice. He also is believed to be the first European to land on the Hawaiian Islands (where he later would be killed) and on Vancouver Island (while searching for a rumored northwest passage between the Atlantic and the Pacific).

"As captain of the Endeavour, he would sight and survey hundreds of landfalls that no Westerner had ever laid eyes on," writes Oliver E. Allen in Pacific Navigators.

> And though the Endeavour would never fire her guns at another ship in battle, Cook's epochal voyage aboard the converted collier was destined to bring under George III's sovereignty more land and wealth than any single naval victory of the powerful British fleet. But the most important prize of this and the two subsequent voyages that Cook would make was measured not in territory but in knowledge.
>
> Patient and methodical where his predecessors had been hasty and disorganized, he would sweep away myths and illusions on a prodigious scale, and in the end would give to the world a long-sought treasure: a comprehensive map of the Pacific.[1]

The British awarded a coat of arms, which included a globe and polar stars, posthumously to Cook. The inscription read, "He left nothing unattempted." He also left very little unfound.

Choosing Your Colonies

Caroline Rodriquez (not her real name) struck a relaxed pose against a nearby pillar in the hotel lobby, but fidgeting hands gave her away. She surveyed the crowd of salespeople gathering anxiously in the lobby, waiting for the trade-show exposition to open. Not that they were all that excited about standing on the carpeted concrete of the convention floor the next three days. Instead, the buzz was about the entertainment scheduled at the end of the industry meeting to follow. The top three salespeople who closed the most sales at the show would win a trip for two to Las Vegas's casinos, with five thousand dollars in gambling money to boot. Even the "losers" would net a night on the town with the some of the raunchiest entertainers in the business.

Caroline should know. It was her budget that would pick up the tab. When her colleagues had first kicked around the sales-incentive idea in the marketing meeting, she had started to speak up with her objections. But as the discussion wore on, Caroline felt uncertain about how to word her reservations. She knew that believers were frequently—and she felt erroneously—labeled as the "against" crowd, and she definitely didn't want to come across as holier-than-thou in her attitude. And she was particularly careful as manager to allow her team as much control as possible.

And yet somebody needed to draw a line in the sand about what was and wasn't appropriate. Precedents preside for a long time. That was the part that concerned her the most. What would they do next year for an encore? How much should she push her views and beliefs about morality on others? Where were the boundaries in a publicly held company? Did she dare speak up?

Creative Colonization Is a Command

Irony is perhaps the only English word that aptly describes the tie that some scholars make between Charles Darwin's theories of evolution and nineteenth-century moralists' rationalization for colonialism.

For a few idealists, the modern era of colonialism—which came in two phases, the first beginning about the time Europe discovered the New World—included a moral element that poet Rudyard Kipling referred to in

1899 as "the white man's burden." Some scholars claim that erroneous generalizations of Darwin's theories supported this justification for colonialism. The idea was that "civilized" people held a moral obligation to govern (and evangelize) primitive cultures of the world. It was their evolutionary right.

However sincere some might have been in this view, the real fuel in the colonization engine was economics, not morality or Darwinism. That was the case when Phoenicians established colonies along the shores of the Mediterranean Sea around 1100 B.C., and it was so when kings and queens (and later presidents) set out to acquire territory halfway around the world. The motive for the European imperialists was to make these foreign lands a source of raw materials and a market (real and potential) for their home-based manufacturers. Trade monopolies that kept exports ahead of imports, according to the theories, would lead to a profitable balance of trade and would fund further expansion.

> The term creative colonization refers to an intentional salt-and-light strategy in any given workplace that identifies spiritual boundaries and presses them to their appropriate limits so that colleagues seriously consider placing Jesus at the hub of their lives.

In its efforts to develop this economic model, Great Britain put its thumbprint on so much of the globe that it once could claim, "The sun never sets on the British Empire." A business trip in 1999 took us around the world—much more quickly, thankfully, than James Cook—that included stops in Vancouver, Hong Kong, Singapore, Malaysia, Bombay, and four cities in India and London. In a span of around two weeks, we had taken a British-crowned colony world tour.

The British impact upon these cities and their countries is indisputable. In some ways, the introduction of foreign customs, plants, and animals wreaked havoc on the indigenous people and their ways of life. In other ways, everyone benefitted. In all ways, things were never the same again. And while the British flag no longer flies above those lands, the British influence is ever present.

There were many traditions and practices that evidenced the lasting result of years of colonization.

In some ways, the follower of Christ today is involved in a similar creative colonization—not in foreign, primitive lands, and not through the use of overbearing, culture-stripping force, but in the high-tech world of the New Economy. The term *creative colonization* refers to an intentional salt-and-light strategy in any given workplace that identifies spiritual boundaries and presses them to their appropriate limits so that colleagues seriously consider placing Jesus at the hub of their lives. The difference, of course, is that commerce doesn't drive the objectives. But there is no better place to accomplish them than in economic settings.

For followers of Christ, colonization isn't just a neat idea—it's a command. Chapters 5, 6, and 7 of the Gospel of Matthew serve as an executive summary of the world's most incredible executive retreat. Think about it. Jesus, the greatest leader of all time, took his leadership team onto a mountain for a few days and essentially gave them a top-line preview of the next two or three years, as well as a behavioral blueprint that we can use to this day.

In Matthew 5:13–16, Jesus told his team, and us:

> You are the salt of the earth. But if the salt loses its saltiness, how can it be made salty again? It is no longer good for anything, except to be thrown out and trampled by men.
>
> You are the light of the world. A city on a hill cannot be hidden. Neither do people light a lamp and put it under a bowl. Instead they put it on its stand, and it gives light to everyone in the house. In the same way, let your light shine before men, that they may see your good deeds and praise your Father in heaven.

In these three powerful verses, Jesus took two household commodities essential to the livelihood of the poorest of the poor and the wealthiest of the wealthy and painted a word picture. Everyone in that culture understood the concept of salt and the concept of light—as does everyone in today's culture.

Jesus was talking about influence. He commanded his followers to have a full and intentional positive influence in their culture. Do all followers of Christ carry out this command? Absolutely not. Their salt becomes tasteless, their light covered or doused. Observation bears this out.

So does the solid research of pollsters like George Barna and George

Gallup Jr. Their respective organizations have tracked religion in America for years. And what are they finding? People continue to believe in God. People are purchasing Christian music and Christian literature as never before. And people are giving money to charities in record amounts. But ethical behavior? Most indicators—the number of school shootings or workplace drug use, for instance—reveal a steady and disturbing decline in Christian colonization.

Gallup, in a 1999 interview with *The Life@Work Journal*, reported that the percentage of American adults who say they want to experience growth in their lives has jumped 24 percent during the last five years, climbing to 82 percent. Sixty percent of Americans still attend a church or some other faith community. And the vast majority of Americans, well over 90 percent, say they believe in God.[2]

But Gallup also recognized that there are at least three "gaps" between what people say and how they live. There's the believing/belonging gap, where people say they believe strongly in something but aren't actively engaged in activities that go along with that belief. They say they are Christians, for instance, but they don't attend church. Second, there is a knowledge gap—the gap between what people say they believe and what they really know about that belief. Third, there's an ethics gap, which is when people's actions don't line up with their professed beliefs.[3]

> Many believers simply aren't doing their part. They aren't having the kind of influence Jesus called them to exert on their culture. They aren't colonizing.

How can this be? Some would argue that there simply aren't enough real followers of Christ, and there's no debating that's part of the problem. Yet it's equally true that many believers simply aren't doing their part. They aren't having the kind of influence Jesus called them to exert on their culture. They aren't colonizing.

How Christ Infiltrates Contemporary Culture

In his classic book *Christ and Culture*, H. Richard Niebuhr explained how our approach to influence grows from our personal definition of our relationship between us and culture. Niebuhr, the son of a German immigrant and himself a professor of ethics at Yale University for many years, outlined five possible scenarios for how followers of Christ interact with culture.[4] They are as applicable today as they were when he wrote them more than fifty years ago.

Christ Against Culture

The people who adopt this method are anticultural, antiestablishment. These radicals want to pull away from society and create a holy huddle or live in a Christian ghetto, where their salt won't be tainted, nor their light challenged. They take an us-against-the-world approach, viewing the world through legalistic, judgmental lens.

Christ of Culture

This stance is the exact opposite of the first one. Instead of rebelling against culture to the point of eliminating all possible contact, these people soak in culture so completely that onlookers stand little chance of distinguishing them from nonbelievers.

Joseph Aldrich, author of *Gentle Persuasion* and *Lifestyle Evangelism*, wrote about this in terms of audience and message. Some believers have a great message, but those who take a Christ-against-culture approach to life have no audience. The Christ-of-culture crowd has plenty of audiences. People love them. But these believers have no meaningful message. They pull the very teeth from the gospel of truth and life. As Niebuhr put it, they have a God without wrath, who brought men without sin, into a kingdom without judgment, through a Christ without a cross.

Christ Above Culture

Most followers of Christ quickly deny this attitude, but many nonbelievers just as quickly identify it in the so-called Christians they know. In a spirit of superiority, these people display an attitude of "I have the truth and you don't." And no matter how you mask it, rename it, or spin it, their attitude still comes across as arrogance.

Christ and Culture in Paradox

This issue deals with a complex ideology of "dualism." Niebuhr points out that these dualists answer the Christ-and-culture questions with a "both/and" response. These proponents don't divide the world into light and dark or the kingdoms of God and Satan. Rather the dualists believe in distinguishing between loyalty to Christ and responsibility for culture, so they squirm in constant conflict between such things as the wrath and mercy of God.

Christ the Transformer of Culture

Christ becomes the colonizer—the salt in the soup, the light in the otherwise darkened alley. With this view, a follower of Christ colonizes his or her segment of the world. Christ painted this picture in the passage we just read: "In the same way, let your light shine before men, that they may see your good deeds and praise your Father in heaven" (Matt. 5:16).

Transformers of Culture

When the British looked for new lands to colonize, they didn't just stick a flagpole in every piece of rock that protruded from the waters of the ocean. They looked for opportunity. They looked for underdeveloped lands that had something to offer them. And, in their view, they looked for lands where they had much to offer the primitive cultures that inhabited them.

> Creative colonization for Christ often takes different forms in different environments, and it seldom looks like the traditional method of preaching fire and brimstone at the water cooler.

Clearly, Jesus calls his disciples to be "transformers of culture." Paul, in his letter to the Philippians, put it this way: "Whatever happens, conduct yourselves in a manner worthy of the gospel of Christ" (Phil. 1:27). No greater opportunity exists in which to live out this command in the modern world than in the marketplace. It's the soup. It's the darkened alley.

For the most part, followers of Christ have a handle on Sunday. There's room for improvement, to be sure. Church growth is slack among many traditional denominations, but more and more churches have identified innovative ways to be culturally relevant and biblically sound. And their members know the part they are called to play on the first day of each week. But many believers never connect the Sunday message to their lives on Monday through Friday in the workplace.

And it is at work, of course, that we spend most of our waking hours. It is at work that most of us are in contact with nonbelievers. It is at work that salt will be most noticeable and that light will shine the brightest.

Work, of course, is a single, definable place in the same way that the Pacific ocean is home to certain fish. But work is much more than a single job. Work includes nonprofit charities, home-based businesses, global conglomerations, privately held factories, publicly traded Internet companies, and government agencies and offices. Each place has its limits, but we must test, push, and challenge those limits. In appropriate ways, of course, but test, push, and challenge nonetheless. Creative colonization for Christ often takes different forms in different environments, and it seldom looks like the traditional method of preaching fire and brimstone at the water cooler.

Here's what it looks like specifically: it is the CEO of a publicly held global Fortune 25 company who pushes the boundaries by inserting his personal testimony into the annual report, checking to see if it's possible to have Christian on-hold music, and allowing a once-a-month luncheon at the corporate office to talk about ethics and excellence in the work environment.

It is the dermatologist who travels to India once a year on a mission trip, covers his office walls with pictures from his trip, and takes the time to explain to inquiring patients exactly why he has a heart for a distant people.

It is a sole proprietor who makes it clear that his commitment to Christ drives him to expend specific energy to hire single mothers in desperate need of a job that pays a good salary and offers a flexible schedule.

It is a division vice president responsible for global operations in a publicly held company who has on his desk a framed copy of his biblically based personal operation principles and who goes over those principles with every new hire who joins the team.

It is the consulting business that takes a portion of its profits each year and splits them among its employees to give to ministry-minded needs around the world.

It is a surgeon who asks her patients if she can pray for them right before the surgery begins.

It is a company that provides scholarships so that its employees can attend seminars such as FamilyLife.

It is the family owned manufacturer that opens chapels in its plants and hires chaplains to minister to the factory workers.

It is the construction company that not only supports overseas missions with money, but also sends its employees into the mission field on a regular basis.

It's the business owner who purposely works to open factories in countries that are closed to missionaries so that his workers can spread the light of Jesus to a workforce living in the dark.

It is the cardiovascular surgeon living by the Golden Rule who has set up a structure that makes it affordable for young doctors to enter the field, joining his staff and having an equal vote in how things are run.

It is the executive vice president of a large HMO who stands up to the CEO, who frequently belittles Christian stances in the organization.

It is the entrepreneur who runs her company by biblical values and principles and lets her employees and clients know that so they can hold her accountable for business practices.

It is the marketing guru who has identified and launched ideas and products and "does deals" with most all the major retail and discount chains in the country to place Christian products on the shelves of their stores.

It is the doctors, nurses, and other staffers at one of the largest cancer centers in the country, telling their patients about the chaplains available to talk to them regarding spiritual needs.

Transformers of culture, every one of them.

Commerce Drives Culture

To change our culture, we must understand what creates it. In earlier times, academicians, family heads, politicians, or spiritual leaders held the reins. At times, the arts and entertainment drove culture, and some might think that's still the case today. Take the business profit out of sports and movies, however, and their influence on culture becomes almost irrelevant. Universities now concern themselves more routinely with which one can create the largest endowments rather than which one can produce the greatest thinkers.

> The global business community, not the church, now sets the moral agenda in the New Economy.

Even churches have discovered that to shape culture, they have to meet the consumer-oriented needs of that culture. Business, which originally followed religious models, now drives religion. The global business community, not the church, now sets the moral agenda in the New Economy.

Equally important to the fact that commerce drives our culture is the road it takes. Postmodern workers, especially those in the younger generations, hunger for a holistic approach in which faith, family, friends, and fun are knitted into the fabric of life. And the common collective fabric of their life is work. That's why they insist that work mean more than a paycheck.

In the November 1999 cover story for *BusinessWeek*, Michelle Conlin summed up the spiritual hunger of the postmodern workforce: "Just as industrialization gave rise to social liberalism, the New Economy is causing a deep-seated curiosity about the nature of knowledge and life, providing a fertile environment for this new swirl of nonmaterialist ideas."[5] The void is undeniable, and like all voids, it is being filled—by a growing number of spirituality-at-work conferences, by books and articles, by small-group discussions and company-sponsored programs on spirituality, and by the influence of individuals within their organizations.

So if followers of Christ want to colonize the world for Christ—if they want to be "transformers of culture"—then their marketplace holds the greatest opportunities.

The Power of One

In many respects, the positive influences Europeans, and later Americans, brought to foreign lands during the heydays of colonization were offset or out-and-out rejected because of the newcomers' methods. Colonizers haven't always been welcomed transformers of culture.

As followers of Christ, we also want our colonization to leave an impact that goes beyond mere tradition—afternoon tea, cricket, left-side-of-the-road traffic. Real salt and real light have a deeper, more meaningful influence. Again, the dilemma for many believers concerns methodology. There are dozens of theories, dozens of methods. Some work; some don't. The ones that work, however, can be boiled down into one basic best instrument of influence: individual, ethical behavior.

This basic tenet of influence is the often-overlooked element of Christ's salt-and-light message—the part that says, "that they may see your good deeds." There's nothing wrong with inviting people to church or to a Bible study. There's nothing wrong with having nonbelieving friends over for dinner or taking them to a nearby theme park to hear a Christian concert. And God will certainly bless those to whom he has given the gift of evangelism. Some people have Scripture verses on their business cards, pass out Bibles on the streets, and press colleagues at the water cooler about where they're planning to spend eternity. But personal evangelism represents only one model of influencing the world for Christ.

According to Jesus' executive briefing—this top-line report direct from the mouth of Jesus to his leadership team—the most effective method of influence is individual, ethical behavior.

Don't misinterpret this conclusion as "works theology" or a "social gospel." It is neither. We're discussing influence, not salvation. And we influence others through individual, ethical behavior: good works, works that are good.

In the Greek, there are two words for "good"—*agathos*, which defines a thing as good in quality, and *kalos*, which means that something is not only good, but also winsome, beautiful, and attractive. *Kalos* is the word Jesus used in Matthew 5:16. As followers of Christ, our behavior, our lives, our works should be *kalos*—winsome, beautiful, and attractive. William Barkley once said that real Christianity is attractive, that it never repels. So it is with ethics in the raw.

> All of us, no matter our age, our spiritual maturity, or our station in life, continually stand at the intersection of right and wrong. Sometimes our decisions are private, sometimes public. But they're always individual choices.

All of us, no matter our age, our spiritual maturity, or our station in life, continually stand at the intersection of right and wrong. Sometimes our decisions are private, sometimes public. But they're always individual choices. Choosing the right thing, over and over and over, results in the Power of One—a strong force for colonization, for transforming culture.

You can see the Power of One in the action of a woman we met not long ago at a community gathering. As she had approached the tollbooth on the turnpike back to Tulsa, she deposited four dollars. As she explained it: "Two dollars for today, and two dollars for that day back in college when I sped through without paying."

You can see the Power of One through an owner of a landscaping business in Florida. When the owner became convicted about his company employing illegal immigrants, he paid for all twenty-five workers to return to Mexico, facilitated their getting the appropriate entry visas, then held their jobs open for them until they returned. To celebrate with them, he invited them as guests to his party, where a Spanish-speaking pastor explained the motivation behind what he'd done. Eleven of the twenty-five prayed to receive Christ into their lives as a result of his act of marketplace integrity.

Kay Coles James demonstrates the Power of One even though her span of influence is not what she expected. When as a housewife and mother she decided America needed a prolife voice on the abortion issue from the African-American community, she agreed to go on television and talk about it. What she didn't realize was that her remarks would be aired in prime time. The debate with callers led to a long-term career in politics, during which she has influenced public policy on several moral issues, serving in the Reagan and Bush administrations as commissioner for the National Commission on Children and Secretary of Health and Human Resources for the Commonwealth of Virginia, and working for the National Right to Life Committee.

The Power of One means a colleague with the gift of evangelism who's always talking about her church events, inviting friends to a Twila Paris concert, and organizing a morning Bible study before the office opens.

The Power of One means someone with the gift of mercy who notices a colleague tearing up in the cafeteria line over an extended illness of a parent and offers a listening ear, Christian counseling, and help with carpooling her children to school.

The Power of One means an employee who shows up for work every day, uses his God-given skills and gifts to serve the company and others, and does his or her work with excellence and with gratitude.

The Power of One means that when you promise to divide profits and pay a bonus, you pay the bonus or commission.

The Power of One means that when a colleague deserves credit for an idea, you give it.

The Power of One means that when you can shave a few dollars off your expenses, you do it.

The Power of One means that when you offend someone and your moral alarm clock goes off, you apologize.

The influence in the marketplace of one individual continually making ethically correct decisions isn't going to triple the value of company stock and it isn't going to turn the workweek into a pleasure cruise. But over time, the practice of individual ethics will have an impact, will make a difference, will provide salt to create a thirst in unbelievers, will release light in the darkness.

The cynic might belittle the idea that the actions of one individual could have an impact on the culture at large. But case after case demonstrates the shallowness of such thinking. You'll recall our earlier story about our con-

> With just a pinch of salt and a candle of light, workers who practice creative colonization could create an avalanche of evangelism.

sulting client, for instance, who was trying to lead his organization into the difficult waters of consolidation. During one meeting, the leadership team discussed an opportunity to purchase a couple of companies. To do so, however, they needed to tighten up their profit-and-loss statements. The solution the president of one division proposed was simple: cook the books. When the chairman said that wasn't possible, the newly hired division president wondered why. A single voice, the chairman responded, "Because it's wrong."

The Power of One. This organization didn't have corporate ethics. It had one individual willing to display ethical behavior.

But can such individual actions influence a crowd of nonbelievers in a marketplace that ignores God? In other words, is the influence welcome? Absolutely. We've worked in hundreds of organizations as consultants, and we have yet to see a boss who didn't welcome someone who wanted to improve the integrity of the company. Strategies for successful companies today do not include working people until they drop dead, lying through negotiations just to make a quick buck, or cheating vendors out of their payment. The ingredients for success in the marketplace today center on building trust and value for all concerned—employees, customers, stockholders. Organizations are begging for employees with integrity—they want to attract them, grow them, promote them, retain them, and count on them to maintain their enthusiasm for the business.

Where the issues of value and trust and integrity surface—and they will surface daily—Christians must engage in the dialogue. That's creative colonization.

During opening remarks at a Promise Keepers rally a few years ago, we stated this belief, one that we still hold today: "If America has a national revival, a turning to God, or back to God, it will not happen through the government venue. It will not happen through the academic venue. It will not even happen through the family. It will happen in the arena of work. That's where salt and light can have its most dramatic effect in both quality and quantity. With just a pinch of salt and a candle of light, workers who practice creative colonization could create an avalanche of evangelism."

Definitely, the salt-and-light command can change our culture, starting in the workplace among the believers. And our churches and spiritual leaders must engage in the dialogue. The New Agers have pulled up a chair to the discussion table. So have the Hindus and the Mormons. Followers of Jesus can no longer hold back. Religious leaders must equip the workers who rub elbows with unbelievers to practice creative colonization. Followers of Christ must understand how their lives can model the message of the Bible every day in every way.

> The single best instrument of influence for a follower of Jesus in the marketplace is individual ethical behavior, day in and day out, in decisions large and small. Individual ethical behavior attracts onlookers.

Michael Novak, author of *Business As a Calling*, once remarked: "This country ought to have, when it is healthy and when it is working as it is intended to work, 250 million policeman—called conscience."[6] He referred to people with the courage and character to make sure that right prevails over wrong. Corporate consciousness and corporate ethical behavior come about only if individuals come together to sprinkle salt and shed light on a bland and dark world. Corporate ethics originate with the Power of One—one person doing ethics in the raw.

To repeat: The single best instrument of influence for a follower of Jesus in the marketplace is individual ethical behavior, day in and day out, in decisions large and small. Individual ethical behavior attracts onlookers. And once nonbelievers are drawn to followers of Christ, the Holy Spirit can open the door wider to reveal the source for that salt and that light—Jesus.

So what next?

• Nail it down. Be a positive influence to colonize your segment of the culture.

• Crank it up. Step up to the window and push the envelope a little. In your work group, in your community, in your industry, with your family, and in your social circles, carry the flag. Whatever your personal style, turn it up a notch. Continue to ask yourself these questions: *Am I doing all I can in my workplace to reveal Jesus in the most public way possible? Do I know what those boundaries look like where I am? Am I pushing the boundaries out as far as is appropriate in my context?*

Colonization will look different in different frontiers. For example, Daniel was quite overt about his beliefs but not inappropriately so. He did not practice in-your-face aggressiveness. But as a result, King Nebuchadnezzar followed God. Nehemiah, on the other hand, displayed a different kind of influence. We don't know how much King Artaxerxes knew about Nehemiah's faith in the beginning, but he eventually found out in the context of the walls being destroyed and rebuilt. Then Paul took an entirely different approach as a missionary.

One size doesn't fit all when it comes to colonization. Whatever your style of evangelism, use it to its limits.

• Live it out. Whatever you do and wherever you work, model the message with your life. Make sure that your ethical choices present an authentic taste test. Many studies have shown that most people do not doubt the existence of God as an idea; what they doubt is that God makes any real difference in a person's life.

Sheldon Vanauken said it so well:

> The best argument for Christianity is Christians—their joy, their serenity, and their completeness. But the strongest argument against Christianity is also Christians. When they are somber, joyless, when they are self-righteous and smug and complacent consecration, when they are narrow and repressive, then Christianity dies a thousand deaths.[7]

We must live our life and work our job in such as way that onlookers observe the message.

As believers, we have won the war; now we just need to occupy the territory.

Through the Power of One, seekers can experience the Power of the One. Colonization then becomes not a forced occupation that yields little lasting impact, but an embraced transfusion of eternal, significant life.

VERY, VERY:
BEING THE BEST IN BOTH WORLDS

ON COOL, CRISP, *cloudless nights, Ferdinand Magellan, one would suspect, took pause on the deck of his ship and gazed up from the unexplored seas and into the unexplored skies. The night lights that hung just beyond the reach of his fingertips helped him plot a course across the Atlantic, down the coast of South America, and through the straits that would connect him to the Pacific, and send him back toward Spain.*

Magellan never made it back; he died during a skirmish with natives on the Philippine Islands. But one of the five ships that began the journey at his command eventually became the first to circumnavigate the globe. It was not Magellan's destiny to complete that trip. But in some ways, the great explorer still is opening the way to new frontiers.

On October 11, 1994, more than four hundred years after a poisoned spear pierced Ferdinand Magellan's skin and took his life, another Magellan—a spacecraft constructed by NASA—plunged into the atmosphere of Venus, earth's sister planet and a light in the heavens that once guided the world's first seafaring explorers. Appropriately, the space shuttle Atlantis *had launched it.*

Magellan *the spacecraft spent four years orbiting Venus, using its sophisticated radar to map 98 percent of the planet's surface before it was intentionally crashed in a suicide mission that would provide reams of fresh data about the planet's atmosphere. Like its namesake, this discoverer confirmed some scientific theories and dispelled many others, proving once again that exploring new frontiers, risky though it may be, is an essential path to truth.*

Traveling the Essential Path

The Chicago meeting brought together about thirty followers of Christ who also happened to be high-level business leaders. They had flown in from all across the country to pursue a greater understanding of servant leadership. But as might be expected from a group with that makeup, the conversation bounced around a variety of topics during the course of the day.

As the meeting wore on, an interesting pattern developed. Whenever the talk focused on business, these leaders dove in with full force and great self-assurance. They talked about P&Ls, marketing strategies, management theories, market trends, branding, and strategic analysis. They reeled off data and statistics the way a baseball fanatic quotes the batting averages of his favorite players.

When the talk turned to theology or Scripture, however, these well-educated, business-savvy leaders invariably prefaced everything they said with an apology: "I'm not a theologian," they would say, "but I think. . . ." Or, "I'm not a professional pastor, but it seems like. . . ." When it was time to talk about business, they were very eager to explain what they *knew*. When it was time to talk about God, they were limited to what they *thought*.

For most of them, it was confidence, not credible content, that they lacked.

Scripture calls us to be "very, very" men and women. Our privilege and responsibility is to be very Bible *and* very business. Many folks we meet are either "very business, sort of Bible" or "sort of business, very Bible." A "very, very" person is one who consistently develops a growing expertise in both Bible and business.

The Fourth Frontier is all about an exploration and understanding of a "very, very" world and becoming a "very, very" follower of Christ—who was very human, very divine—with both confidence and credibility. When we explore devotion, calling, integrity, stewardship, rest, and colonization, and begin to put into practice the principles we learn there, our actions—our lives—become "very, very." Because the Fourth Frontier is such an unexplored territory, however, there aren't many "very, very" people around. And therein lies the challenge for every follower of Christ who reports to work in the New Economy.

Don't think we're denigrating the business leaders who gathered in Chicago. We're not. Go to any pastors' conference in the country and survey the clergy, and you'll likely find the opposite side of the coin. You'll find men and women who speak with passion and authority about the Bible, but who hem and haw about the world of work. Or go to any city in America and randomly pick a focus group from people who regularly attend a mainstream church. Very few, if any, will have a "very, very" approach to life, and some won't even consider that a goal.

Know the Book; Live the Book

New believers are the only people with a legitimate reason to say, "I don't know the Bible very well." Anyone who has been in the faith for a few years ought to know the Book, regardless of whether he or she receives a paycheck from a church or has attended seminary. The accountant should know Numbers as well as she knows numbers. The attorney should know Judges as well as he knows judges. And the politician should know First and Second Kings as well as he knows the modern kings.

But we don't live in that world of "very, very" believers.

Gary M. Burge, writing for *Christianity Today*, pointed out that comedian Jay Leno once couldn't find anyone in his audience who knew even one of the Ten Commandments, but he had no trouble finding folks who could identify all four members of the Beatles. A sad statement on our secular culture? No, a sad statement on our culture—period. As Burge went on to point out in "The Greatest Story Never Read," even incoming freshmen at Bible colleges—kids who for the most part attend church regularly—fared poorly when tested on their biblical knowledge.[1] Biblical illiteracy, as all the surveys bear out, grows worse in America with each passing day. Thus nonbelievers lose valuable insights into the many great works of literature that allude to the Bible. And believers miss out on the overt—not to mention the subtle—nuances that run like a thread from Genesis through Revelation.

A life with Christ, of course, centers on a relationship, not legalism. The invitation to accept Christ and walk with him does not specify a number of hours each week that we should spend memorizing Scripture. But Jesus is called the Word (John 1), and the Word is something you read, something you memorize, something upon which you meditate. And if our goal is to be Christlike, we must look at his model. He knew the Scriptures not because of legalism, but because of relationship. Scripture was and is one critical way to better know God.

And yet this directive doesn't mean that all followers of Christ should pack their collective bags and head for seminary. The writer of Hebrews put it thusly: "May the God of peace, who through the blood of the eternal covenant brought back from the dead our Lord Jesus, that great Shepherd of the sheep, equip you with everything good for doing his will, and may he work in us what is pleasing to him, through Jesus Christ, to whom be glory for ever and ever. Amen" (Heb. 13:20–21).

Jesus was "very, very." He was the God-man, very human, very divine. When people try to make him one or the other, not only do they violate good biblical theology but they end up creating some sort of schizoid Jesus. The Lord wasn't "sort of human, very Godlike" or "very human and kind of Godlike." He wasn't an "okay carpenter" and a "great rabbi." The Greek word *tekton* used in Mark 6:3 to describe Jesus refers to someone who was more than an average carpenter of the time but a skilled craftsman, capable of creating pieces that were both practical and beautiful. Jesus was indeed an excellent carpenter who turned out an excellent product at a profit, and he was indeed a divine servant of God while in the marketplace. He was all mortal and all immortal at the same time. He was "very, very," and so, too, should we strive to hit that target.

> We must strive to become "very, very"—to go to the arena that's filled with fans and competitors, not the stadium that sits silent and empty on a cold, dark night.

It's very possible to be in the business world and serve money while thinking you're serving God. And it's also very possible to be in the church world and think you're serving God while you're serving your own ego. That delusion is a pitfall in both worlds.

The most effective agent of salt and light in the New Economy is a follower of Christ who embodies a "very, very" mindset and a "very, very" lifestyle—a person firmly planted in professional excellence and deeply rooted in biblical truth. Why? Because that combination represents the momentum of culture, where a biblical mandate crosses with a cultural hunger, where the dialogue is taking place, where the game is being held. As men and women who long to walk more closely with Christ, to represent him as good and faithful servants, we must strive to become "very, very"— to go to the arena that's filled with fans and competitors, not the stadium that sits silent and empty on a cold, dark night.

Bob Briner, the longtime president of ProServ Television, came face-to-face with the difficult nature of this task. From humble beginnings, Bob worked his way through the ranks in the highly competitive world of professional sports, working in the front office of the Miami Dolphins before launching a career as an agent and then as a television producer. He traveled the world, mingling with some of the wealthiest people on the planet. But he found himself woefully unprepared to integrate his faith in Jesus with his work.

"As I searched for help in combining Christian living with my world of professional sports and television, it didn't come from my church or denomination," Briner wrote in *Roaring Lambs,* a groundbreaking book challenging believers to impact culture through their work. "And in fairness to this great group of believers, I have not found much help in this area from any of the other traditional evangelical groups."[2]

Briner, who died in 1999 at age sixty-three, set out to become a "very, very" person by infiltrating the culture through his work. As an influential force in the world of professional sports, television, and business, he intentionally, overtly, and skillfully melded the world of Scripture with the world of daily living, and he did it in a profession that isn't exactly known for its overwhelming acceptance of believers in Jesus. When he met with the Shah of Iran, he wanted to evidence Christ. When he negotiated with Akio Morita, the legendary founder of Sony, he wanted to represent Christ.

His passions included a strong concern that nonbelievers see Jesus in everything we do, especially the skill and excellence of our work. But while schools and professional associates trained him well to excel in his work, he didn't find much training on how to be a follower of Jesus—unless he wanted to become a pastor or a missionary or the leader of a parachurch organization; unless he wanted to pack up and move to what he called the "Christian Ghetto." The church, Briner noted, "is almost a nonentity when it comes to shaping culture. In the arts, entertainment, media, education, and other culture-shaping venues of our country, the church has abdicated its role as salt and light."[3]

And the same could be said of the executive suites, the small businesses, the professional offices and every other area of work—from Silicon Valley to Wall Street, from masonry to manufacturing, from plumbing to podiatry.

Churches have led a wonderful movement in the last twenty years to do a better job of connecting with the culture in general. People have called them "seeker-friendly" and "purpose-driven" churches. In our opinion, the next step in the progression is the "very, very" church.

The church of the future must adapt a new structure that targets the Monday-through-Friday side of life, a new strategy that embraces a "very, very" style of ministry. The "very, very" church will focus where people really traffic, where they really do salt and light. Its pastors will interact regularly with their congregations during the workweek—not just at the hospital bedside, but in the board room and on the factory floor.

At the dawn of this realization, many pastors today are making the shift to more effective marketplace ministry. In former days, pastors who preached sermons about work could talk about it only as it related to church committees or offices or service on a church staff. But today pastors are expanding their ministries and messages to be more appropriate to the typical worker out in the world.

For example:

PASTOR A (Traditional Minister)	PASTOR B (Marketplace Minister)
Portrays Bible characters as those in bedtime stories	Presents Bible characters in all their humanity and struggles
Explains theology without application	Explains theology through application to real work-life situations
Uses illustrations from his personal life and those from others in the professional ministry (pastors, missionaries, evangelists, authors, theologians)	Uses illustrations from believers in the church who are living their faith successfully outside the church walls
Provides all the answers, regardless of the questions	Asks the relevant questions to earn the credibility and platform to provide the right answers

When conflict arises between church activities and work schedules, asks business leaders to choose the church because it is the first priority	When there's a conflict between church activities and work schedules, asks business leaders to use their God-given talents in the marketplace where they serve the largest audiences
Invites business leaders to advise him on how better to run church programs and ministries	Observes business leaders in their workplace to understand and advise them on what the Bible says about dilemmas they face
Encourages members to bring their friends to church	Encourages members to take the message of the gospel to their friends
Spends time with the well-known and powerful people so that their association can lend credibility to the message of his sermons	Spends time with the "average" people so that his sermons can encourage and build credibility in them to expand their influence to nonbelievers in the marketplace
Organizes programs to train people to serve better in the church	Organizes programs to train people to use their spiritual gifts for service to others in the marketplace, community, and family
Talks about what's important in the church and his ministry	Asks about what's important in members' lives and how he can encourage and help them be salt and light in their world

A nationwide study of preaching by the University of Wisconsin-Oshkosh found that a majority of ministers and priests are not yet communicating effectively, which no doubt helps explain why attendance is down for most houses of worship. "Listeners are begging for relevancy, and they're not getting it," Lori Carrell, the communications professor who conducted the study, told the *Milwaukee Journal Sentinel*. "They want to be lifted up. And if they do want any kind of change, it's application, it's personal. Like, 'What should I do on Tuesday morning when faced with this decision?'"[4]

How did we in today's churches get into this predicament? We've had a flip-flop on emphasis. Thirty years ago, churches emphasized content, not life experience—anecdotes and feelings were irrelevant. And when churches focus on content without experience, they foster a dry, legalistic understanding of Scripture. The Pharisees and Sadducees had content, but little understanding. Jesus castigated them continually for passing tests of content down to the minutiae when they showed no mercy or compassionate understanding.

Yet when churches focus solely on experience, as many do today, followers of Christ walk away with exuberance and uplifting motivations, but with little understanding of biblical content, little understanding of the how-to's for living out their commitment.

The typical follower of Jesus in the workplace often has no idea how much the Bible has to say about all the decisions, dilemmas, deals, and duties he or she faces every day at work—from handling change to coping with trauma, from creating a strategic plan to managing a staff dispute, from establishing travel policies to dealing with a dishonest supervisor. The Fourth Frontier includes an underdeveloped gold mine, with nuggets of truth on making career moves, getting and applying guidance, casting a vision, hiring good people—in short, every aspect of work. The Bible contains solutions to the whole of life's problems, including those at work. But few people make the connection.

> The typical follower of Jesus in the workplace often has no idea how much the Bible has to say about all the decisions, dilemmas, deals, and duties he or she faces every day at work.

"Very, very" means that we as believers in the marketplace need to focus on both content and experience. As workers, we need to connect Sunday to our Monday-through-Friday worlds. We can't be role players about our faith; we can't be bluffers. We have to know, understand, do. And it also means that we, and our pastors, must connect the Monday-through-Friday life back to a Sunday world. We must close the circle, connecting God's influence *on* our lives back to God's influence *in* our lives.

When that happens with individuals, personal lives and families change. When it happens with the masses, the world changes.

The Second Reformation

The current spiritual awareness in the Fourth Frontier has the potential to initiate nothing short of a second reformation, a new swelling of the pioneer spirit. The first Reformation changed not only the church but also the world. Why? Because God was smack-dab in the center of it. The Fourth Frontier gives believers the opportunity to revitalize culture by once again putting God smack-dab in the center of it.

The Reformation, widely regarded as the most important religious happening of the second millennium, traces its roots to Germany, where Johann Gutenberg invented and developed the printing press in the mid-fifteenth century and where Martin Luther nailed his ninety-five theses to the door of the church in Wittenberg in 1517.

Interestingly, economics partly drove that Reformation. To raise funds, Pope Leo X began selling "indulgences." Need to get Cousin Ed out of purgatory? No problem. Worried about your future sins? No problem. Randy Alcorn, in his book *Money, Possessions and Eternity*, points out that when Johann Tetzel came to town "selling forgiveness as if it were a sack of potatoes or a pair of shoes" on behalf of the pope, a local priest became fed up with the system. That priest was Martin Luther.[5]

> What's new isn't the availability of Scripture to the common citizen, but the application of Scripture to the common life—all areas of it.

Luther, John Calvin, and others provided the message, and Gutenberg provided the means to distribute it. The world would never be the same.

No reasonable person can separate the advancements of the Enlightenment—the progress made in science, in medicine, in education, in theology, in the arts—from the Reformation. During the first Reformation, these changes became reality largely because of the insatiable interest in Scripture. Thanks to Gutenberg's printing press, the Bible finally became accessible to the common person. The average person could read and understand it; that change became the catalyst for life coming together in ways almost incomprehensible to us today.

Think about it: People were living in the "dark ages" of civilization. They lived in ignorance, with little or no authority, freedom, autonomy, or permission to develop a personal relationship with Jesus Christ based on the content of his revelation in Scripture. Then someone put Bibles in their hands and said, "See for yourselves!" The Bible became the tool that all people of all nations at all times could hold in their hands and say, "This has connection to my world."

People searched for God, and culture—all of humanity—reaped the benefits.

Such dramatic change did not happen in the seventh century when people worshiped crystals; it happened when truth began to permeate all areas of life. When God's truth and life are not confined to a box, then big things happen, change beyond human explanation.

Although creativity, innovation, and discovery remain a part of our world, in many arenas, man has put God back in his box. People seem determined to go it alone, to use only human intellect and skill while plumbing the house, selling the toys, managing the project team, operating on the sick, sculpting the statue, researching the cure for disease, or drafting the design for an office building or cathedral. But when we include God—when we live a "very, very" life—the big becomes bigger, the great becomes greater, the impossible becomes possible.

The second reformation can herald the same dramatic change. Again, we see an insatiable interest in Scripture, but this time with an eye toward its application in our professional work life, a frontier where biblical knowledge and influence have been seriously lacking. What's new isn't the *availability* of Scripture to the common citizen, but the *application* of Scripture to the common life—all areas of it. We have a new opportunity to bring God out of the box (as if mortals could keep him there!) and experience his wonders at work in the marketplace.

A New Age Ripe for Influencing: The New Manifesto of the Main Economy

Never before has our culture been more receptive to the influence of believers on behalf of God's kingdom. Why? Because of the increasing entrepreneurial approach to work. People want a stake in the product they're creating or the service they're providing. Along with that desire, they have a mindset to accept higher risks. They have the capacity to share in the downside of their decisions as well as the upside. It would not be much of an overstatement to say that in Silicon Valley, employers cannot hire someone unless the new employee will share equity in the company. This new mindset remains just one more undeniable reality of the holistic approach to life.

In light of this new reality, consider for a moment these observations about changes materializing today. We call it the Manifesto of the New Economy.

Formerly, to have influence a worker had to be at the top of the hierarchy. If lower in the organization, he or she had to go through the chain of command to be heard or to work as part of a team to shake the ladder above. Today, because of the Internet, the individual can connect with anyone—upward, downward, and laterally—to influence change.

Power to the Idea

Formerly, workers had to catch the attention of someone higher up the ladder to gain an audience for their ideas. Lacking that platform of credibility, they had to pass their ideas from boss to boss to boss. By the time the idea surfaced at the top, it often had taken on a new flavor, and everyone else took part of the credit. Today, good ideas themselves can gain attention.

Power to the Individual

The motto was, "New ideas are a dime a dozen; success turns on the implementation." Today, the competitive advantage rests on new ideas, never mind the implementation. Being first with an idea will grab market share; somebody later will work out the bugs.

Power to the Follower

Formerly, people didn't have a choice about whom they followed. They looked for the person higher on the ladder and followed with their heads down. Today, seniority has lost its status. Workers follow whom they will—those with the best ideas, strongest track record, and highest integrity. Leadership skills used to be defined by and taught to only the executives. Today, in many organizations, every single employee receives leadership training. The operative word is *influence*, not *directive*. If leaders don't lead, workers don't follow. That mindset of choice deposits power in the hands of followers.

Power to the Leader

Formerly, leaders issued directives. Workers followed these directives often in letter, but not in spirit. Enthusiasm about following the leader? Forget it. But today, when a worker chooses to follow a leader, that leader has even greater power than before. Because of the holistic approach to life, that follower is open to influence in all areas of life, including personal, family, and religious. The passion with which people today choose to follow gives an entirely new meaning to the old fishing cliché, "We've got them, hook, line, and sinker."

Power to the Hobby

Formerly, people worked at a job because it paid well or brought status. Then they spent their leisure time playing at their hobbies or moonlighting with a job or volunteer activity they enjoyed. Today, people are looking for ways to make their passion their work and work their passion. "Live your dream, and the money will follow" has become the heartfelt theme of a larger portion of the population. As a result, people have identified and followed their passion, giving them a sense of wholeness and satisfaction never before experienced. Where their heart is, there they find their treasure.

Power to the Globe

Formerly, the typical worker interacted only with other people working down the hall or across town. Even if a worker had enormous charisma, he or she could expect to influence only people in close physical proximity. But with today's technology, workers can exert their influence around the globe. By way of e-mail, Internet, intranets, video-conferencing, and satellite broadcasts, workers can share their ideas and expand their influence to Dubai as well as Denver, Kosovo as well as Cleveland. In other words, today we have the potential to see good news—the real Good News—travel around the globe before we can take off our glasses.

> Every worker—CEO or clerk, rich or poor, healthy or sick, attractive or homely—can carry a big spotlight and a big salt shaker to shine and sprinkle around the globe.

Because of this New Manifesto of the Main Economy, our age has become pregnant with potential for ushering in a new foundation for life: God. In short, every worker—CEO or clerk, rich or poor, healthy or sick, attractive or homely—can carry a big spotlight and a big salt shaker to shine and sprinkle around the globe. The Power of One: one person can single-handedly shake up an entire global system for soul-searching work.

Consider the first Reformation again. The theological movement of the time is often summed up in the "five *Sola*":

- *Soli Gracia*—Grace Alone (salvation comes by the grace of God alone)
- *Soli Scriptura*—Scripture Alone (the Bible as the inerrant and infallible)
- *Soli Fide*—Faith Alone (justification is by faith alone)
- *Soli Christo*—Christ Alone (Jesus is the only way to God, to truth, and to eternal life)
- *Soli Deo Gloria*—Glory to God alone (everything to the glory of God)

It is that last *soli* that's still waiting to happen. *Soli Deo Gloria* is all about giving God alone the glory—in everything. Not just singing God's praises once a week at a church service. Not just praising God for the birth of a child. Not just staring in wonder at the trees in the forest or the stars in the sky. To God alone the glory—as a mechanic, a CEO, an artist, an attorney, and a pastor. It's a "very, very" way of thinking, a "very, very" way of working, a "very, very" way of living.

The Variables of "Very, Very"

The first Reformation basically freed people to pursue salvation by faith without works. The second Reformation frees us to pursue a career calling from Christ without guilt. We are free from the sacred/secular dichotomy. We are free from the tyranny of thinking that the only spiritually significant work is traditional vocational ministry. We are free from thinking that our lives need to be divided into departments in order to be biblical. In traditional thought, family is big, church is big, work is small. The second Reformation frees us from that misperception.

With this freedom, a variety of opportunities present themselves. All sorts of benefits surface. We can experience the breadth, depth, and width of God's work in our world. We can acknowledge and connect with him in the arena where we spend most of our time and where our greatest gaps exist. The believer is blessed. God is honored.

With this connection comes renewed wonder and awe for a God who is in control of the smallest details of our world and who cares about every aspect of our lives—from the color we paint our house to the way we compose our e-mail. God is not a detached, uncaring Creator who left us to our own devices. Rather, we understand that God loved us so much that he became "very, very" and provided what Satan thought was impossible—a perfect sacrifice for sins—ours and those of the world.

From that wonder and awe for God comes a sense of confidence and security about life, not to mention a sense of fulfillment and contentment about our work. When we are free to pursue God *and* our professional career—not either/or—we are free to work with more passion than ever before, to be content in the understanding that we might serve God and glorify God better as a carpenter than as a youth counselor.

We develop a "very, very" understanding of discipleship and evangelism. As followers of Christ, we aim to experience God and grow in his grace (discipleship). And we purpose to introduce that love and light to other people (evangelism). For the most part, however, we have been doing evangelism and discipleship over, under, around, and without the work component. Yet it is in the work world that we receive our most rigorous training in discipleship (where we experience God and grow in his grace). And it is in the work world that we find our best platform for effective evangelism. A "very, very" life gives meaning to those realities and energizes us for those opportunities.

> Clearly there's a spiritual hunger in our world unlike that at any other time in history, a searching for meaning among the lost, and a longing for direction among the found.

With that confidence, with that sense of contentment, we can energetically embrace the Fourth Frontier adventure. What can be more thrilling than exploring and gaining new understanding about God's plan for his people? What can be more exciting than God doing his work through us?

Entering the Fourth Frontier

Clearly there's a spiritual hunger in our world unlike that at any other time in history, a searching for meaning among the lost, and a longing for direction among the found. The evidence—the indisputable desire among people to live a more holistic life—suggests that God is presenting his people with still another opportunity to connect more closely with him.

At the core of the first Reformation was a broadening awareness of God-activity, of God-connection. We are coming to see that connection again and igniting a second reformation. As a "very, very" follower, your challenge is this: develop devotion. Identify your calling. Live with integrity. Practice stewardship. Rest to reflect. Colonize creatively.

If we understand that God matters to our work, then we understand the driving force for the exploration of the Fourth Frontier—the pursuit of a life with Jesus. We as explorers seek first his kingdom and his righteousness in ways that acknowledge our work as part of his grand plan, just as he laid it out for us before we discovered the first frontier. The marketplace, the Fourth Frontier, is about doing *our* work on *his* behalf.

Engage in the dialogue. Exert your influence. Enjoy the journey.

NOTES

Chapter 1
1. Os Guinness, *The Call* (Nashville: Word Publishing, 1998), 172.
2. Dorothy L. Sayers, *Creed or Chaos* (Manchester: Sophia Institute Press, 1974), 76–78.
3. Ibid., 77.
4. Gerald Zelizer, "Businesses Seek Religion to Improve Bottom Line," *USA Today,* 17 November 1998, page 27A.
5. Michelle Conlin, "Religion in the Workplace: The Growing Presence of Spirituality in Corporate America," *BusinessWeek*, 1 November 1999, 152.
6. Raid Gauloises website: *http://www.raid-gauloises.com*
7. Ibid.

Chapter 2
1. Daniel J. Boorstin, *The Discoverers* (New York: Vintage Books, 1983), 219–220.
2. C. S. Lewis, *The Collected Works of C. S. Lewis.* Inspirational, 1996, 223.
3. Peter Drucker as quoted in Bill Moyers, *A World of Ideas* (New York: Doubleday, 1990), 408.

Chapter 3
1. Boorstin, *The Discoverers*, 159.
2. Ibid., 162.
3. Paul Bernstein, *American Work Values.* State University of NY Press, 1997, 5–7.
4. Nancy Caver, "Prayers and Poultry: Tyson Execs Give the OK to Bring Religion into the Workplace," *Arkansas Democrat-Gazette*, 29 January 2000, 4–5B.
5. Ibid.
6. Michelle Conlin, "Religion in the Workplace: The Growing Presence of Spirituality in Corporate America," *Business Week*, 1 November 1999: 153.
7. Kirk Livingston, "Construction Zone," *Life@Work* 3, no. 2 (March/April 2000): 39.
8. Ibid., 38.

Chapter 4
1. T. S. Eliot, *The Waste and Other Poems* (San Diego: Harcart Brace & Company), 1934, 46.

2. Stephen Moore and Julian L. Simon, "The Greatest Century That Ever Was: 25 Miraculous Trends of the Past 1000 Years," *Policy Analysis* (The Cato Institute), no. 364, 15 December 1999, 69.
3. Michelle Martinez, "DuPont Program Beats the Winter School's Out Dilemma," *HR Magazine,* June 1997.
4. Robert Neeley Bellah, ed., *Habits of the Heart: Individualism and Commitment in America* (Berkeley: University of California Press, 1996), 43.
5. Guinness, *The Call,* 4.
6. Boorstin, *The Discoverers,* 251.

Chapter 5
1. Saint Augustine, *Confessions,* trans. Henry Chadwick (Oxford: Oxford University Press, 1991), 24.
2. Ibid.
3. Ibid., 104.
4. Ibid., 153.
5. "America's Christian Commitment Has Remained Relatively Stable for the Past Decade," 1 September 1999; Barna website: *www.barna.org*
6. Ibid.
7. "Teenagers Embrace Religion But Are Not Excited About Christianity," 10 January 2000; Barna website: *www.barna.org*
8. Ibid.
9. Ibid.
10. Ibid.
11. Christa Ehmann, "The Age Factor in Religious Attitudes and Behavior," 14 July 1999; Gallup website: *http://www.gallup.com/poll/releases/pr990714b.asp*
12. Saint Augustine, *Confessions,* 91.

Chapter 6
1. *www.matthewhenson.com/discovered.htm*
2. Guinness, *The Call,* 4.
3. Stephen Caldwell, "Finding Your Job Fit," *Life@Work* 1, no. 3 (August 1998): 24.

Chapter 7
1. Irving W. Anderson, "The History of the Lewis and Clark Expedition," Lewis and Clark Trail Heritage Foundation, Incorporated: *http://www.lewisandclark.org*
2. Ibid.
3. *www.pbs.org/lewisandclark/archive/idx_jou.html*

4. Kenman Wong, "Finding True North," *Life@Work* 2, no. 5 (September/October 1999): 48.

5. "Omni Hotels Removes Adult Movies From Guest Room Televisions," press release, 5 November 1999; website: *www.omnihotel.com*

6. Dallas Willard, Laura Nash, and Millard Macadam, "Searching for an Ethical Base," *Life@Work* 2, no. 5 (September/October 1999): 62.

7. Ibid.

Chapter 8

1. *The London Times,* as quoted in Jon Krakauer, *Into Thin Air: A Personal Account of the Mount Everest Disaster* (New York: Villard, 1997), 18.

2. Frederick Buechner, *The Hungering Dark* (San Francisco: HarperSanFrancisco, 1969), 73.

3. Robert R. Ellis, "Divine Gift and Human Response: An Old Testament Model for Stewardship," *Southwestern Journal of Theology*. 32, no. 2, Spring 1995, 4–5.

4. Randy Alcorn, *Money, Possessions and Eternity* (Wheaton, IL: Tyndale House Publishers, 1984), 172.

5. Stephen Caldwell, "The Servant General," *Life@Work* 1, no. 6 (November/December 1998): 19.

6. Ibid., 18.

Chapter 9

1. Kirk Livingston, "Tackling Torque," *LifeWork* 2, no. 4. (July/August 1999): 32.

2. Wayne Muller, *Sabbath: Restoring the Sacred Rhythm of Rest* (New York: Bantam Books, 1999), 2–3.

3. Nancy Ann Jeffrey, "Sleep: The New Status Symbol," *Wall Street Journal,* 02 April 1999, w1.

4. Ibid.

5. Abraham Joshua Heschel, *The Sabbath: Its Meaning for Modern Man* (New York: Farrar, Straus and Giroux, 1995), 3.

6. Muller, *Sabbath: Restoring the Sacred Rhythm of Rest*, 1.

7. Livingston, "Tackling Torque," 34.

8. Stephen Caldwell, "Off The Fence," *Life@Work* 2, no. 4 (July/August 1999): 54.

9. Muller, *Sabbath: Restoring the Sacred Rhythm of Rest*, 1.

10. Abraham Joshua Heschel, *The Sabbath: Its Meaning for Modern Man*, 6.

11. Wallace Stevens. "An Ordinary Evening in New Haven." Michael Griffith. "The Religion, Literature and the Arts Nexus in Australia in the 1990s (an edited version of a paper delivered at the 1995 AASR

Conference at Australian Catholic University, Aquinas Campus, Ballarat). http://www.acu.edu.au/rla/nexus.html, 5.

12. Charles W. Colson, *Born Again.* (Grand Rapids, MI: Flemming H. Revell Co., 1995), 93

13. Ibid.

Chapter 10

1. Oliver E. Allen, *Pacific Navigators* [publishing info], [page number].

2. Stephen Caldwell, "The Inner Frontier," *Life@Work* 2, no. 5 (September/October 1999): 35.

3. Ibid., 38.

4. H. Richard Niebuhr, *Christ and Culture* (New York: Harper Torchbooks, 1951), vii.

5. Conlin, "Religion in the Workplace, 156.

6. Michael Novak, *Business As a Calling* (New York: The Free Press, 1996), 377.

7. Sheldon Vanauken. *A Severe Mercy.* (New York: Harper & Row, Publishers, Inc. 1977), 85.

Chapter 11

1. Gary M. Burge, "The Greatest Story Never Read," *Christianity Today.*

2. Bob Briner, *Roaring Lambs* (Grand Rapids: Zondervan Publishing House, 1993), 15.

3. Ibid., 28.

4. Tom Heinen, "Sermons Often Disappoint, UW-Oshkosh Prof Says: Few Preachers Consult with Congregation Members," *Milwaukee Journal Sentinel*, 7 January 2000, B–5.

5. Alcorn, *Money, Possessions and Eternity*, 78, 84.

INDEX for *The Fourth Frontier*

How can you blend biblical wisdom with business excellence?

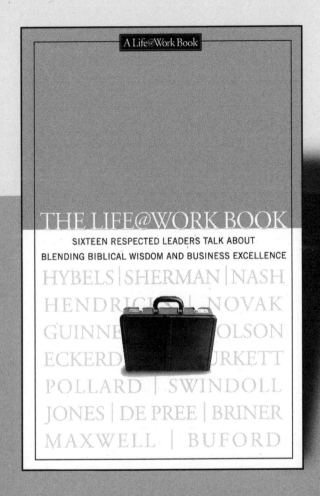

A Life@Work Book

THE LIFE@WORK BOOK

SIXTEEN RESPECTED LEADERS TALK ABOUT
BLENDING BIBLICAL WISDOM AND BUSINESS EXCELLENCE

HYBELS | SHERMAN | NASH
HENDRICKS | NOVAK
GUINNESS | COLSON
ECKERD | BURKETT
POLLARD | SWINDOLL
JONES | DE PREE | BRINER
MAXWELL | BUFORD

john**maxwell**

bill**hybels**

charles**colson**

larry**burkett**

charles**swindoll**

bob**buford**

lauriebeth**jones**

doug**sherman**

william**hendricks**

michael**novak**

os**guinness**

jack**eckerd**

laura**nash**

william**pollard**

max**depree**

bob**briner**

Learn from 16 respected leaders as the award-winning *The Life@Workbook* journal brings together, for the first time, the most intriguing and insightful writings of their contributors in one incredible volume.